PU

ROBO

You are a rancher in the land of Thalos. You p
enemies, the savage Karosseans – have built huge robots for many purposes: mining ore, erecting buildings, moving cargo, and herding the vicious dinosaurs that live on Thalos.

One morning you discover that all your colleagues have been overcome by a strange sleeping sickness and you are unable to rouse them. Then you hear a rumble overhead. In the clear blue sky you see the unmistakable shape of a Karossean robojet! You realize that the protection of your homeland against the deadly Karosseans and marauding dinosaurs is up to YOU alone!

Two dice, a pencil and an eraser are all you need to embark on this thrilling adventure, which is complete with its elaborate combat system and a score sheet to record your gains and losses.

Many dangers lie ahead and your success is by no means certain. It's up to you to decide which route to follow, which dangers to risk and which adversaries to fight!

Fighting Fantasy Gamebooks

1. THE WARLOCK OF FIRETOP MOUNTAIN
2. THE CITADEL OF CHAOS
3. THE FOREST OF DOOM
4. STARSHIP TRAVELLER
5. CITY OF THIEVES
6. DEATHTRAP DUNGEON
7. ISLAND OF THE LIZARD KING
8. SCORPION SWAMP
9. CAVERNS OF THE SNOW WITCH
10. HOUSE OF HELL
11. TALISMAN OF DEATH
12. SPACE ASSASSIN
13. FREEWAY FIGHTER
14. TEMPLE OF TERROR
15. THE RINGS OF KETHER
16. SEAS OF BLOOD
17. APPOINTMENT WITH F.E.A.R.
18. REBEL PLANET
19. DEMONS OF THE DEEP
20. SWORD OF THE SAMURAI
21. TRIAL OF CHAMPIONS

Steve Jackson's SORCERY!

1. THE SHAMUTANTI HILLS
2. KHARÉ – CITYPORT OF TRAPS
3. THE SEVEN SERPENTS
4. THE CROWN OF KINGS

FIGHTING FANTASY – The Introductory Role-playing Game

OUT OF THE PIT – Fighting Fantasy Monsters

Steve Jackson and Ian Livingstone
present:

ROBOT COMMANDO

Steve Jackson

Illustrated by Gary Mayes

Puffin Books

Puffin Books, Penguin Books Ltd, Harmondsworth, Middlesex, England
Viking Penguin Inc., 40 West 23rd Street, New York, New York 10010, U.S.A.
Penguin Books Australia Ltd, Ringwood, Victoria, Australia
Penguin Books Canada Limited, 2801 John Street, Markham, Ontario, Canada L3R 1B4
Penguin Books (N.Z.) Ltd, 182–190 Wairau Road, Auckland 10, New Zealand

First published 1986

Made and printed in Great Britain by
Cox & Wyman Ltd, Reading
Filmset in Linotron Palatino by
Rowland Phototypesetting Ltd,
Bury St Edmunds, Suffolk

Dedicated to my grandparents,
E. B. and Bonnie Lairmore

With special thanks to the playtesters:
Monica Stephens, C. Mara Lee, Jerry Self,
Norman Banduch, Jim Gould, Allen Varney,
Creede and Sharleen Lambard

CONTENTS

INTRODUCTION

To play this game, you will need a pencil, an eraser, and two ordinary six-sided dice. You will also need the *Adventure Sheet* on pp. 22–3. You are advised either to use a pencil when writing on the *Adventure Sheet*, or to make photocopies of these pages to use in future adventures.

Skill, Stamina and Luck

Before embarking on your adventure, you must first determine your own strengths and weaknesses. You must use the dice to determine your *Initial* SKILL, STAMINA and LUCK scores. On the *Adventure Sheet* you will find boxes for recording each of these three scores.

Roll one die. Add 6 to this number and enter this total in the SKILL box on the *Adventure Sheet*.

Roll both dice. Add 12 to the number rolled and enter this total in the STAMINA box on the *Adventure Sheet*.

Roll one die. Add 6 to this number and enter this total in the LUCK box on the *Adventure Sheet*.

For reasons that will be explained below, SKILL, STAMINA and LUCK scores change constantly during an adventure. You must keep an accurate record of these scores. For this reason, you are advised either to write small in the boxes or to keep an eraser handy. But never rub out your *Initial* scores. Although you may be awarded additional SKILL, STAMINA and LUCK points, these totals may never exceed your *Initial* scores unless something specifically occurs to change your *Initial* scores.

Your SKILL score represents your general fighting expertise, both with your own weapons and when you are piloting a robot. Your STAMINA score reflects your general constitution, your will to survive, your determination and overall fitness. Your LUCK score indicates how naturally lucky a person you are. The higher each of these scores, the better!

Robots

If you are familiar with the Fighting Fantasy Gamebook series, you know most of the rules. But robots will be new to you.

There are many different types of robot, and you will have a chance to pilot them all. You may use any robot you find. However, you may have only one robot at a time! Each robot's abilities are determined by several scores:

ARMOUR represents the robot's toughness and ability to take damage. This is like your own STAMINA score. A robot has an ARMOUR score *instead* of a STAMINA score.

SPEED tells how fast a robot can travel. This gives an

advantage in combat. A faster robot has a +1 bonus to its SKILL against a slower opponent. Robots may be Slow, Medium, Fast, or (for flying robots) Very Fast. If your robot is slower than the enemy you are fighting, you may never *Escape*, even if the page offers you that option!

COMBAT BONUS: When you use a robot, you fight with your own SKILL. But some robots are especially made for battle, and give you a COMBAT BONUS when you fight. Some robots are especially *unsuited* for battle, and you will have to *subtract* points from your SKILL!

SPECIAL ABILITIES: These are different for every robot. When you get a robot with a useful special ability, you should either make a note of it, or write down the number of the paragraph that describes the robot, so that you can double-check if need be.

Possessions

At the beginning of the adventure, your only Possessions are your sword and five medikits for curing wounds. As the adventure progresses, you will lose or use up some Possessions, and gain others. All Possessions should be recorded in the appropriate box on the *Adventure Sheet*.

Unless the description of an artefact says *specifically* that it must be mounted permanently on a robot, you may carry all artefacts with you when you leave a robot.

When you pick up an interesting artefact, you should make a note of the reference where you found it, just in case you have to check later to see exactly what it does. Note also that the *names* and *model numbers* of artefacts may contain clues. Always write down the full name and number of anything you pick up, including robots!

Individual Combat

You will often come across pages in the book which instruct you to fight a foe of some sort. An option to flee may be given, but if not – or if you choose to attack the foe anyway – you must resolve the battle as described below. This procedure is used when you, personally, face an opponent. (For battles you fight while piloting a robot, see below on Robot Combat.) It is the same system that is used in other Fighting Fantasy books; you can skip this section if you are already familiar with the rules.

First, record the foe's SKILL and STAMINA scores in the first vacant Encounter Box on your *Adventure Sheet*. The scores for each foe are given in the book each time you have an encounter.

The sequence of combat is then:

1. Roll both dice once for the foe. Add its SKILL score. This total is the foe's Attack Strength.
2. Roll both dice once for yourself. Add the number rolled to your current SKILL score. This total is your Attack Strength.
3. If your Attack Strength is higher than that of the foe, you have wounded it. Proceed to step 4. If the foe's Attack Strength is higher than yours, it has wounded you. Proceed to step 5. If both Attack Strength totals are the same, you have avoided each other's blows. Start the next Attack Round from step 1 above.
4. You have wounded the foe, so subtract 2 points from its STAMINA score. You may use your LUCK here to do additional damage (see below).
5. The foe has wounded you, so subtract 2 points from your own STAMINA score. Again you may use LUCK at this stage (see below).
6. Make the appropriate adjustments to either the foe's STAMINA score or your own (and to your LUCK score if you used LUCK – see below).
7. Begin the next Attack Round by returning to step 1. This sequence continues until the STAMINA score of either yourself or your foe has been reduced to zero (death) – or until you *Escape*.

Robot Combat

These are the rules for battling dinosaurs and giant robots. Whenever you are fighting in your robot – and whenever the opponent has SKILL, ARMOUR and SPEED scores instead of just SKILL and STAMINA – then the rules for robot combat must be used. They are very similar to the normal combat rules, as follows:

1. Roll both dice once for the foe. Add its SKILL score. Add 1 if the foe is *faster* than your robot. This total is the foe's Attack Strength.
2. Roll both dice once for yourself. Add the number rolled to your current SKILL score. Add any COMBAT BONUS that was listed for the robot you are piloting. Add 1 if your robot is *faster* than the foe. This total is your Attack Strength.
3. If your Attack Strength is higher than that of the foe, you have wounded it. Proceed to step 4. If the foe's Attack Strength is higher than yours, it has wounded you. Proceed to step 5. If both Attack Strength totals are the same, you have avoided each other's blows. Start the next Attack Round from step 1 above.
4. You have wounded the foe, so subtract 2 points from its ARMOUR score. You may use your LUCK here to do additional damage (see below).
5. The foe has wounded you, so subtract 2 points from your own robot's ARMOUR score. Again you may use LUCK at this stage (see below).
6. Make the appropriate adjustments to either the

foe's ARMOUR score or your own robot's ARMOUR score (and to your LUCK score if you used LUCK – see below).

7. Begin the next Attack Round by returning to step 1. This sequence continues until the ARMOUR score of either yourself or your foe has been reduced to zero (see below) – or until you *Escape*.
8. If your foe's ARMOUR is reduced to zero, you have won. If your own robot's ARMOUR is reduced to zero, it has been destroyed. But *you* are not necessarily dead, or even injured. You do not lose any of your own STAMINA unless the instructions specifically say so. You may have a chance to survive and continue your adventure in another robot.

Escaping

On some pages you may be given the option of running away from a battle should things go badly for you. However, if you do run away, the foe automatically gets one wound on you (subtract 2 STAMINA or ARMOUR points) as you flee. Such is the price of cowardice. Note that you may use LUCK on this wound in the normal way (see below). You may only *Escape* if that option is specifically given to you on the page, *and* if your robot is *faster* than your foe.

Fighting More Than One Foe

If you come across more than one opponent in a particular encounter, the instructions on that page will tell you how to handle the battle. Sometimes you must fight them all together; sometimes you will fight each one in turn.

Luck

At various times during your adventure, either in battles or when you come across situations in which you could either be lucky or unlucky, you may call on your LUCK to make the outcome more favourable. But beware! Using LUCK is a risky business, and if you are *un*lucky, the results could be disastrous.

The procedure for using your LUCK is as follows: roll two dice. If the number rolled is equal to or less than your current LUCK score, you have been Lucky and the result will go in your favour. If the number rolled is higher than your current LUCK score, you have been Unlucky and you will be penalized.

This procedure is known as *Testing your Luck*. Each time you *Test your Luck*, you must subtract 1 point from your current LUCK score. Thus you will soon realize that the more you rely on your LUCK, the more risky it will become.

Using Luck in Battles

On certain pages of the book you will be told to *Test your Luck* and will be told the consequences of your being Lucky or Unlucky. However, in battles, you *always* have the option of using your LUCK, either to inflict a more serious wound on a foe you have just injured, or to minimize the effects of a wound the foe has just inflicted on you.

If you have just wounded the foe, you may *Test your Luck* as described above. If you are Lucky, you have inflicted a severe wound and may subtract an extra 2 points from the foe's STAMINA or ARMOUR score. However, if you are Unlucky, the wound was a mere graze and you must restore 1 point to your opponent's STAMINA or ARMOUR (i.e. instead of scoring the normal 2 points of damage, you have now scored only 1).

If the foe has just wounded you, you may *Test your Luck* to try to minimize the wound. If you are Lucky, you have managed to avoid the full effect of the blow. Restore 1 point of STAMINA or ARMOUR (i.e. instead of doing 2 points of damage it has done only 1). If you are Unlucky, you have taken a more serious blow. Subtract 1 extra STAMINA or ARMOUR point.

Remember that you must subtract 1 point from your LUCK score each time you *Test your Luck*.

Restoring Skill, Stamina and Luck

Skill

Your SKILL score will not change much during your adventure. Occasionally, a page may give instructions to increase or decrease your SKILL score. An increase in SKILL may be general, affecting all combats, or it may affect only one type of combat. Your SKILL score can never exceed its *Initial* value. However, bonuses (from artefacts or robots with a COMBAT BONUS) can add to your SKILL no matter how high its level is.

At the beginning of the game, your SKILL is the same in all situations. However, various artefacts may increase your SKILL for one type of combat but not the other. For instance, a sword of high quality might increase your SKILL for personal combat but not for robot combat – the sword is of no use when you are piloting a robot!

Stamina

Your STAMINA score will change a lot during your adventure as you fight various foes and undertake arduous tasks. As you near your goal, your STAMINA level may be dangerously low and battles may be particularly risky, so be careful!

When you start your adventure, you will have five 'medikits'. Each medikit can be used to restore 1 lost point of STAMINA. Cross each one off your *Adventure Sheet* as it is used. You are assumed to carry these with you at all times. However, they may not be used during a battle – only afterwards! Remember also that your STAMINA score may never exceed its *Initial* value.

Luck

Additions to your LUCK score are awarded when you have been particularly lucky, or when you do something deserving of luck. Details are given in the pages of the book. Remember that, as with SKILL and STAMINA, your LUCK score may never exceed its *Initial* value.

HINTS ON PLAY

In this book, you will become a lone guerrilla, fighting against a horde of invaders. There are three entirely different ways to defeat the invaders – one obvious, the others not so obvious! Each method requires a different path, different artefacts and different decisions.

You are advised to make faithful notes about the places you visit and the things you learn; they could save your life. You will sometimes have the chance to go back to a place you have already visited during the same adventure. In any event, your notes will be useful in further adventures, enabling you to pass rapidly on to unexplored places.

You may also want to make a map of the countryside as you pass through it. In particular, it will help you to learn the relative positions of the cities you visit.

Not every spot that you visit will be helpful; some contain only traps and foes which you will no doubt fall foul of. Many wrong turnings are possible . . . and, even if you reach the ultimate destination, you may not have everything you need to succeed.

It will be realized that the entries make no sense if read in numerical order. It is essential that you read only the entries you are instructed to read, starting with the Background and entry **1**, and continuing from there.

The one best path to victory may not be the obvious one – but it requires a minimum of risk. Any player, no matter how weak on *Initial* dice rolls, should be able to use any of the three strategies fairly easily once the best path has been discovered.

Good luck!

ADVENTURE SHEET

SKILL	STAMINA	LUCK
Initial Skill=	*Initial Stamina=*	*Initial Luck=*

POSSESSIONS

Sword

Five Medikits

YOUR ROBOTS

Armour = *Speed =* *Combat =* *Bonus =*	*Armour =* *Speed =* *Combat =* *Bonus =*	*Armour =* *Speed =* *Combat =* *Bonus =*
Armour = *Speed =* *Combat =* *Bonus =*	*Armour =* *Speed =* *Combat =* *Bonus =*	*Armour =* *Speed =* *Combat =* *Bonus =*

ENCOUNTER BOXES

Skill= *Stamina=*	*Skill=* *Stamina=*	*Skill=* *Stamina=*
Skill= *Stamina=*	*Skill=* *Stamina=*	*Skill=* *Stamina=*
Armour = *Speed =* *Combat =* *Bonus =*	*Armour =* *Speed =* *Combat =* *Bonus =*	*Armour =* *Speed =* *Combat =* *Bonus =*
Armour = *Speed =* *Combat =* *Bonus =*	*Armour =* *Speed =* *Combat =* *Bonus =*	*Armour =* *Speed =* *Combat =* *Bonus =*

BACKGROUND

You are a rancher in the land of Thalos. Your people (and your enemies, the savage Karosseans) have built huge robots for many purposes. With a skilled operator at the controls, a robot can replace a hundred men – to mine ore, erect buildings, – move cargo, or just about anything else.

The robots are also your best defence against the vicious dinosaurs of Thalos. Many years ago, the great lizards caused much destruction. But now mankind has learned to tame the beasts, and many of the folk of Thalos – like you – are dinosaur ranchers. The ranchers use Mark 5A utility robots, known as 'cowboys', to herd the dinosaurs! But

wild dinosaurs are still dangerous, and all robots have guns to defend themselves.

Early one morning, you are just finishing your breakfast when one of your assistants staggers into the kitchen. 'So sleepy,' he says. Then he sits down at the table, pillows his head on his arms and goes to sleep!

You shake him, but you cannot rouse him. Alarmed, you go for help. But everyone else you see is asleep.

You rush back inside and switch on a radio. But you can get only scraps of messages: 'Everybody asleep . . . Karossean attack . . . can't stay awake . . .' Soon there is nothing to be heard. You go outside again and pour cold water on several of your friends – but they just snore and mutter.

Then you hear a rumble overhead, like thunder out of the clear sky. You look up. Streaking overhead is the unmistakable shape of a Karossean robojet!

You realize what must have happened. Somehow, the Karosseans have managed to put everyone in Thalos to sleep . . . everyone but you. For some reason, you are immune.

Over the next few hours, you listen to the enemy communications and piece together the story. In the past, the Karosseans had steered clear of Thalos; with its brave warriors and its many robots, your land was too tough to attack. But Minos, their leader, hit on a clever plan. His spies spread capsules of a virulent sleeping sickness – and before long, all Thalos was asleep!

Soon you hear a broadcast from Minos himself, talking to his invading troops. An élite force of a thousand warriors, with hundreds of robots, has invaded Thalos. But this is only the beginning. With the population helpless, Minos plans to loot your country. Its riches and its robots will be his; its people will be sold as slaves! And only you can stop it . . .

You know what you have to do. You walk back inside and buckle your father's old sword to your waist. Food will be no problem – you know supplies will be easy to find – but you pick up a supply of five

medikits. Then you head for the robot parking-area. Alone, you must defeat the Karossean invaders and free your land!

NOW TURN THE PAGE

1

At the robot parking-area, you stop and look around. There are several robots there, but only two seem suitable for long-distance travel. You study them both. If you want to take a standard 'cowboy' walking robot, which is not fast, but sturdy and adaptable, turn to **24**. If you would prefer a light flyer, which is very speedy and manoeuvrable, but not really intended for combat, turn to **47**.

2

'Insufficient data,' replies the computer. 'Probability of Karossean trick 67 per cent. You have five seconds to change your course.' If you continue talking to give the computer guardian more data, turn to **357**. If you turn your robot and go elsewhere, turn to **376**.

3

Because you are not familiar with this type of robot, you do not get the normal COMBAT BONUS with it – in fact, your SKILL is 1 *less* than usual while you use it. You realize you had better get out of there while you can. Turn to **147**.

4

The main encampment of the Karosseans is easy enough to find; they have taken over the city stadium. Even from a distance you can see flying robots wheeling overhead. If you approach in your robot, turn to **18**. If you go on foot, turn to **32**.

5

Your path takes you across a shallow swamp; the road is narrow, and the ground to either side looks soft and sticky. When you round a corner, you see a large dinosaur ahead of you. It is not a flesh-eater, but it does not seem disposed to get out of your way. If you fight it, turn to **239**. If you leave the road, turn to **95**.

6

A blast from the Supertank cracks the pilot's compartment of your robot and vaporizes everything within. You came close to winning and, even in defeat, you shattered the enemy invasion force – but your adventure is over.

7

You give the proper countersign. The Karossean sentry radios you back: 'Pass, friend!' You have fooled him! You can go about your work. Where were you when you were challenged:

The City of Knowledge? Turn to **63**
The City of Industry? Turn to **132**
The Capital City? Turn to **222**

8

The sea-coast is a narrow strip of sand, bounded on one side by the ocean and on the other side by steep cliffs. After a few minutes of travel, you see something ahead. It is a huge herd of Brontosaurus dinosaurs. Most of them are munching on seaweed thrown up by the storms, but a few are investigating something that glitters. If you investigate it yourself, turn to **84**. If you turn around and go back to the city, turn to **144**.

9

There are several robots here, all identical. They are similar to the Cowboy Robot that you used on your ranch, but more heavily armed and armoured, for use against the largest dinosaurs. These Super-Cowboy Robots move by walking. Each has weapons almost as powerful as those of a war robot.

SUPER-COWBOY ROBOT

ARMOUR 14 SPEED Medium

COMBAT BONUS +1

SPECIAL ABILITIES: This robot carries a 'Sonic Screamer' weapon designed to distract dinosaurs. Reduce the SKILL of any enemy dinosaur by 1 when you fight it in the Super-Cowboy. Unfortunately, the special weapon is no use against other robots.

You may take one of these robots if you like. If you had a robot already, make a note that this is where you left it. What will you do now:

Get in your robot and cross the electro-fence? Turn to **129**
Go to the Administrative Building? Turn to **85**
Leave the Dinosaur Preserve? Turn to **150**

10

You decide to visit the Capitol Building, the seat of government of Thalos. If you go in your robot, turn to **42**. If you travel on foot, turn to **71**.

11

The hospital is crawling with Karosseans, both soldiers and doctors. By hiding and skulking, you manage to snatch two medikits. You cannot risk staying longer. Carefully, you slip out of the hospital and away. Return to **308**.

12

You are now flying above the city. The storm is incredibly violent. You cannot control your flyer! Roll two dice. If the result is less than or equal to your SKILL, turn to **316**. If the result is more than your SKILL, turn to **379**.

Gary Mayes

13

You enter the village and investigate. You find one useful robot, a Digger Robot. This slow but powerful machine rides on treads. It has a bulldozer blade on the front, a scoop-shovel on the back, and two large claws for lifting.

DIGGER ROBOT

ARMOUR 16 SPEED Slow COMBAT BONUS 0

SPECIAL ABILITIES: The digger robot can try to strike with the scoop-shovel. This is a clumsy attack (−2 to your roll), but if it succeeds, the foe takes 6 points of damage!

If you do not have a robot, you take the Digger Robot. If you already have a robot, you may pick which one to continue with. You set your course once more for the City of Knowledge. Turn to **361**.

14

You stay in your robot and travel to the huge Thalian Museum. This is the largest museum in all the land; it is full of exhibits on every imaginable subject. If you have been here before, turn to **160**. If you have not been before, continue reading.

As you approach the museum, you keep a sharp watch, but you see no enemies. When you arrive, you park your robot in front of the building and walk up the steps, past a pair of carved stone dragons. The museum attendant is snoring, but the little Information Robot is alert. 'Can I help you?' it asks. What will you do:

Ask for military information? Turn to **36**
Ask for information on sleeping sickness? Turn to **80**
Ask for information on the Karosseans? Turn to **58**
Leave the museum? Turn to **102**

15

The tunnel goes lower and lower into the earth. Then it opens into a wide, dimly lit vault. If you enter the vault, turn to **340**. If you continue downwards, turn to **178**.

16

You turn north through the deserted city. You see few people lying in the streets here; thinking of the jungle so close by, you shudder. You fear you know what has happened to the people here. Then, rounding the corner, you see that you were right. A Nothosaurus is coming towards you, long tongue flickering. This dinosaur walks on all fours or swims in shallow swamps. It is both a predator and a scavenger. If you flee immediately, turn to **331**. Otherwise, fight the creature:

NOTHOSAURUS

ARMOUR 7	SPEED Slow	SKILL 9

If you kill the Nothosaurus, turn to **51**. If your own robot's ARMOUR is reduced to 0, turn to **279**. If you *Escape*, turn to **331**.

17

If you know what you might find in this building, add 50 to its model number and turn to that paragraph. If this means nothing to you, return to **85**.

18

If you fly towards the enemy encampment, turn to **55**. If you travel on the ground, turn to **187**.

19

You hear a crashing sound in the jungle, coming towards you. It is a low, armoured dinosaur, waving a club-like tail back and forth. It is coming straight at you. If you flee, turn to **115**. If you attack the dinosaur, turn to **400**.

20

The whole sixth floor of the Centre seems to be a cross between a laboratory and a gymnasium. In the middle of the room is a device like a suit of armour. Beside it is a sleeping fellow, somewhat battered around the face, in an athletic suit. After a little investigation, you find that the device on the floor is an experimental 'Amplifier Suit', designed to make its wearer almost as strong and fast as a robot. If you want to try it on, turn to **83**. If you want to try another floor instead, turn to **333**.

21

You flee in fear out of the temple. You can feel the disapproval of the Powers of Glory. Lose 1 LUCK point and 1 SKILL point for your cowardice. Return to **166**; you may not visit this temple again.

22

You use the code-words you found with the map reference. 'Acceptable,' crackles the voice of the guardian computer. 'Entering at Clearance Level Zero.' Turn to **175**.

23

Unfortunately, this experimental craft is different from all other robots you have handled. Its COMBAT BONUS of 2 does *not* count for you until you have been through two combats with it. Turn to **378**.

24

This man-shaped robot is designed for dinosaur herding. It moves by walking. It has weapons for dealing with rogue dinosaurs, but they are not as powerful as those of a war robot.

COWBOY ROBOT

ARMOUR 10	SPEED Medium
COMBAT BONUS 0	SPECIAL ABILITIES: None

Now you must choose a place to go: turn to **70**. If you change your mind and want to take the flyer instead, turn to **47**.

25

This is the Robot Experimental Centre. If you have been here before, turn to **251**. If you have not been here before, keep reading. You know little about the Centre except its name, but you have heard rumours that top-secret work is being done here. Turn to **333**.

26

You are being attacked by a Karossean Air-Fighter! This is a sleek, arrow-shaped robot. It can sprout legs to land on the ground, but it always fights in the shape of an aircraft.

AIR-FIGHTER

ARMOUR 7 SPEED Fast SKILL 9
SPECIAL ABILITIES: None

If you defeat the Air-Fighter by reducing its ARMOUR to 0, turn to **113**. If your own robot's ARMOUR is reduced to 0, turn to **136**.

27

This Karossean robot is like nothing you have encountered before. It is a Crusher, a humanoid robot, but twice as large as those you have seen before. It has no guns, but was designed for destroying forts and trenches. It attacks by stamping with its huge feet.

CRUSHER

ARMOUR 14 SPEED Slow SKILL 8

SPECIAL ABILITIES: Although the Crusher is not especially skilful, every time it hits it does *double damage*. Thus, it does 4 with a normal strike, or 2 if you use LUCK successfully, or 6 if you try LUCK and fail!

You cannot *Escape*. If you destroy the Crusher, turn to **275**. If it reduces your ARMOUR to 0, turn to **384**.

28

You quickly activate the controls to turn your robot into its flying form. The transition, usually so swift, seems incredibly slow in the face of the rampaging herd . . . but in the nick of time you swoop away. If you wait until the dinosaurs have dispersed, then land to see what they were looking at, turn to **62**. If you go back to the city, turn to **144**.

29

You put on the Cloak of Invisibility and explore the hospital. Although the building is full of enemies, the Cloak lets you pass among them without being spotted. You find a robot surgeon which heals your wounds: restore your STAMINA to its *Initial* level. You also find two medikits in an unguarded room. You find nothing else of any particular use. At length, your Cloak begins to flicker; you will not be able to use it again. You return to your robot. Turn to **308**.

30

You have defeated the Tripods, but you hear more enemies on the way. You have time for only one choice. If you examine the wreckage of the Tripods, turn to **68**. If you enter the fuel plant, turn to **132**.

31

You decide to explore the streets of the Capital City. How will you travel:

Flying about?	Turn to **55**
Ground travel, going left?	Turn to **153**
Ground travel, going right?	Turn to **290**

32

If you possess the Cloak of Invisibility and have not used it, turn to **90**. Otherwise, turn to **103**.

33

Giving the odd-looking plant a wide berth, you continue on your path. Turn to **237**.

34

You decide to wander around and see what you can find. The streets are choked with huge vehicles, stranded where they fell or rolled when their pilots went to sleep. If you explore to the east, turn to **342**. If you go west, turn to **195**.

35

You have defeated the Karossean ambush. All three robots lie smashed and burning on the ground. What will you do:

Explore the city?	Turn to **366**
Explore the jungle?	Turn to **170**
Leave the city?	Turn to **298**

36

'Well, that depends on what kind of information you need. Modern military information is classified, and you would have to ask at the War College. Historical military information is in Hall Beta. We have some wonderful exhibits.' If you go to Hall Beta to look at the military exhibits, turn to **146**. If you ask for something else, turn back to **14**.

37

Your prayer is quickly answered. A blanket of peace comes over you . . . the same peace that the other worshippers received. You feel yourself falling asleep. Perhaps the Powers of Peace will protect you from the Karosseans somehow, but your adventure is over.

38

If you are travelling on the ground, turn to **137**. If you are flying, turn to **313**.

39

After several hours of travel, you enter rocky terrain. The path narrows, and you are forced to use both of your robot's hands just to climb. You wish you were in a vehicle that could just fly over all this! Suddenly, you hear a roar. Looking behind you, you see a huge Tyrannosaurus sprinting through the rocks at you! Jaws agape, it lunges towards you, and robot and dinosaur fall to the ground, grappling fiercely. This huge meat-eater is the 'king of the dinosaurs', and attacks anything it sees to feed its savage appetite. You must fight it to the finish.

TYRANNOSAURUS

ARMOUR 8 SPEED Fast SKILL 9
SPECIAL ABILITIES: None

You cannot *Escape*; the Tyrannosaurus is faster than you are, and it is familiar with the territory. If you defeat the Tyrannosaurus, turn to **235**. If it reduces your robot's ARMOUR to 0, turn to **258**.

40

You have returned to the City of Knowledge. In the distance, you see the towers of the College of Medicine. But you also see a Karossean air-fighter, closing fast! If you know a password with which to challenge the enemy, turn to that number. If you do not know the password, turn to **305**.

41

At the airfield, you find dozens of pleasure craft of all sorts, none of which looks useful. But parked in an out-of-the-way corner is a small but deadly-looking fighting-machine. It is a sleek experimental fighter, called a Wasp Fighter. Only a few exist. It has very little armour, but it has good weapons and handles well.

WASP FIGHTER

ARMOUR 6 SPEED Very Fast COMBAT BONUS 2
SPECIAL ABILITIES: Whenever the Wasp's Attack Roll exceeds its foe's roll by 4 or more, it has literally flown circles around its foe! It automatically wins the *next* combat round as well – no rolls are necessary.

You may take it if you like. If you return here later, your old robot will be here instead of the Wasp. Return to **165**.

42

The closer you get to the building, the more Karosseans you see. Soon you realize that your robot is making you far too conspicuous. Turn to **71**.

43

You are leaving the City of Storms. Where would you like to go:

The City of Knowledge?	Turn to **361**
The City of Worship?	Turn to **166**
The City of the Guardians?	Turn to **1XX**

Note that you cannot visit the City of the Guardians until you know the numbers to use in place of 'XX'.

44

The lift doors clang shut and it begins to descend. After about five minutes, it stops again. Outside is a corridor even dimmer than the area you just left. The door opens just wide enough for you to squeeze out. Will you press another button (turn to **269**), or step out and go down the corridor (turn to **15**)?

45

You return to the robot that brought you to the city. You collect your Possessions and climb out of the one you used in the jungle. Just as you reach the ground, you hear a thunderous explosion. You have been ambushed! Your old robot is going up in flames. Behind you, guns are firing at the one that took you through the jungle. If you climb back into that robot and fight, turn to **347**. If you run for cover, turn to **159**.

46

You charge to the attack! The Karossean controlling the other robot is caught totally by surprise. Roll two dice and do that much damage to the enemy robot before its pilot can react. If you roll 12, turn to **109**. Otherwise, turn to **78**, mark off the damage you did, and fight.

47

This flying robot, called a Dragonfly Model D, looks like a gigantic dragonfly, complete with buzzing wings. Its main advantage in combat is its speed.

DRAGONFLY MODEL D

ARMOUR 5 SPEED Very Fast COMBAT BONUS 0

SPECIAL ABILITIES: Because this craft is so manoeuvrable, you can escape from *any* opponent – even another 'Very Fast' one – if given the option to *Escape*.

Now you must choose a place to go: turn to **70**. If you change your mind and want to take the Cowboy Robot instead, turn to **24**.

48

You step over the fragments of the smashed robot and enter the laboratory. Inside, you find something very interesting: the prototype for a Seeker Missile. There is only one, but it looks very handy. It can be attached to the outside of any robot. It can be used only when you are piloting a robot – not in personal combat. It may be fired at any time, *between*

Attack Rounds. It will automatically hit its target and reduce its ARMOUR score by 10.

As you take your prize downstairs, you see another Guard Robot like the one you defeated. You hurry out of the lobby and back to your robot. You may install the Seeker Missile now, or save it for another robot. It may be moved from one robot to another, but it is lost if the robot carrying it is lost, or if it is fired. Turn to **206**.

49

Which temple would you like to visit:

The Temple of Peace?	Turn to **365**
The Temple of Fear?	Turn to **304**
The Temple of Nothingness?	Turn to **249**
The Temple of Glory?	Turn to **339**

50

The Karossean troops, already nervous because of the reports of Thalian robots at large, don't hesitate. They set off a buried mine, placed beneath the gate as a precaution. Your robot is shattered. Your adventure is over.

51

You have destroyed the scavenging Nothosaurus. Add 2 LUCK points for protecting the sleeping people from this menace. If you have not already explored the south of the city, you may do so (turn to **225**). Otherwise, turn to **137**.

Gary Mayes.

52

You've fought robots, and you've fought dinosaurs, but this hybrid foe is too much for you. The beating your robot took has injured you: lose 2 STAMINA points. As your battered robot pulls away, you hear the mechanical Tyrannosaurus give a mechanical scream behind you. You had best go elsewhere; you don't want to be here when the Karosseans come to find out what has happened! You leave; you may not return to the museum again. Turn to **63**.

53

In a closet, you find what appears to be an unused coat-hanger – but when you pick it up, it is heavy! You have found the Cloak of Invisibility. Inside it are the instructions. When it is activated, it will cause light waves to pass around you, making you invisible for about an hour. But it will only work once without being recharged, and the instructions do not say how to recharge it. Return to **85**.

54

You are at the College of Medicine. This is both the greatest hospital and the greatest medical laboratory of your entire nation. You approach cautiously, but see no sign of the Karossean invaders. You leave your robot near the front steps and enter the building. If you have been here before, turn to **232**. If you seek treatment for your own injuries, turn to **77**. If you look for information on sleeping sickness, turn to **126**.

55

Your robot takes to the air, and you can soon see the enemy encampment. But the enemy air patrols are vigilant: two flying robots swoop to challenge you. They do not ask for a password, but open fire immediately. You must fight these two Myrmidon robots. The Myrmidon is the standard Karossean combat robot. It has two forms – humanoid and fighter-plane. These two are in plane form and will not try to change during the battle.

First MYRMIDON
ARMOUR 8 SPEED Very Fast SKILL 11
Second MYRMIDON
ARMOUR 8 SPEED Very Fast SKILL 9
SPECIAL ABILITIES: None

If you defeat the two Myrmidons, turn to **75**. If they defeat you, turn to **125**. If you *Escape*, turn to **98**.

56

You have defeated the Ankylosaurus. Looking along the trail of destroyed vegetation that it left behind, you see a glint of metal. If you investigate, turn to **263**. If you ignore it and go on, turn to **321**.

57

Soon your robot is parked in front of the Temple of Fear. It is a huge, irregularly shaped building, built entirely from black stone. Within it are served the Powers of Fear. If you are having second thoughts about your visit, you may return to **166**. If you wish to go inside, turn to **193**.

58

'Oh, very good,' the little robot responds. 'We have a wonderful exhibition on Karossean history and culture in Hall Epsilon.' If you go to Hall Epsilon to study Karossean history, turn to **124**. If you would rather ask for something more up to date, turn back to **14** and make another choice.

59

Before long, you have put the equipment to work on your own robot. Restore your robot's ARMOUR score to its *Initial* value. As you finish your work, the machines' programming powers them down. You try, but you cannot restart them. You may not return here for further repairs. You find nothing else of interest in the shop. Turn to **110**.

60

You can tell that your robot is nearly done for. If you would like to bail out of your crippled machine, turn to **183**. If you would rather fight to a finish, return to **341** and complete the battle.

61

Your luck can't last for ever, since you are without a robot in a hostile city. Eventually you are spotted and captured. When your countrymen awake, they join you in the slave-pens. Some day you may escape, but for now your adventure is over.

62

The dinosaurs were investigating a Cowboy robot – possibly belonging to their herder – which is half buried in the sand. The machine proves to be unsalvageable, but within its cockpit you find two medikits. You may add these to your Possessions and continue. You cannot return to the seashore. Turn to **144**.

63

Where would you like to go:

The Thalian Museum?	Turn to **160**
The College of Medicine?	Turn to **54**
The College of War?	Turn to **277**
The Dinosaur Preserve?	Turn to **66**
Out of the city?	Turn to **380**

64

You set off into the jungle – a brave move, but a foolish one! A prowling dinosaur snaps you up so quickly that you hardly have time to realize your danger. Your adventure is over.

Gary Mayes.

65

You park your robot beside the door and enter the College of War. You are alert for other Karosseans, but apparently the sentry outside was the only one. The halls and rooms are littered with beribboned generals, fast asleep.

Following the signs, you head for the library to see what you can learn. But, just as you get there, you hear a roaring sound from outside. Looking out of the window, you see three sleek fighter-planes hurtle down, sprout legs and turn into robots like the sentry outside. The Karosseans are arriving in force!

You quickly look around the room. There are several volumes on the counter, as though someone was trying to check them out just before the sleeping sickness hit. The books are too large to carry, and you have time to look at only one. Which title will you choose:

The City of the Guardians? Turn to **256**
Emergency Procedures? Turn to **300**
Karossean Military Robots? Turn to **268**

66

You are at the entrance to the Dinosaur Preserve, where some of the wildest and most vicious creatures of all Thalos are kept for study. If you have already been here, turn to **189**. Otherwise, keep reading.

An electro-fence keeps the creatures from rampaging out. On your side of the fence is cool green grass;

on the other side is rank jungle. Also on your side of the fence are two buildings: the Administrative Building, and a huge, unmarked, barn-like structure. What will you do:

Leave your robot and go to the Administrative Building? Turn to **85**
Leave your robot and go to the other building? Turn to **171**
Stay in your robot and cross the electro-fence? Turn to **129**
Leave the Dinosaur Preserve? Turn to **150**

67

Storm clouds are gathering as you approach. But even through the static on your radio, you can hear chatter in Karossean voices. Then you are challenged by several Karosseans in small robots. If you fight them, turn to **217**. If you fly away from them, turn to **12**.

68

You check the wrecked Tripods. You are in luck! Thanks to their modular design, one has a piece of undamaged armour-plate that will fit any robot. You can attach it now, or save it until later (though you may not install it during a battle). It will restore 1 point of ARMOUR, though this may not raise your robot's ARMOUR score above its *Initial* score. It may be used only once! Turn to **293**.

69

You leave the building on foot. The smashed remains of your robot lie in the street outside; the ones you fought are nowhere to be seen. You will have to explore the city on foot in hope of finding something. You cannot go to another city until you find a robot; if you have to fight a dinosaur, you will be in trouble! Where will you go:

The north part of the city? Turn to **16**
The south part of the city? Turn to **225**
The jungle? Turn to **64**

70

Now what are you going to do? You know that, although there are probably Karosseans everywhere, their base is at the Capital City. But you can't just charge in there and attack them with your little robot! You must prepare well before you make your move. Fortunately, there are many cities in Thalos. You will be able to search the whole country for help, if need be, before you confront the invaders. Two large cities are fairly close. If you want to go to the City of Knowledge, turn to **93**. If you want to go to the City of Industry, turn to **209**.

71

You decide to go on foot. If you possess the Cloak of Invisibility and have not used it, you may use it now: turn to **106**. If you have already used it, do not possess it, or if you simply choose not to use it, turn to **134**.

72

The tunnel continues on and levels out again. Lose 1 STAMINA point. Eventually it opens up into a large area filled with dimly visible hulks. Turn to **340**.

73

Almost immediately the path forks again. To the left, a large sign reads 'Danger! Man-trap!' There is no sign by the right path. If you go left, turn to **128**. If you go right, turn to **188**.

74

If you seek treatment for your own injuries, turn to **219**. If you look for information on sleeping sickness, turn to **395**.

75

You have eliminated the two enemy robots – but at a cost. You are somewhat shaken up by the manoeuvres you have been forced to perform; lose 1 STAMINA point. More foes are approaching rapidly. If you press on towards the encampment, turn to **245**. If you retreat, turn to **98**.

76

You continue through the enemy encampment. Soon you can see the wide barrier separating the main encampment from the Karossean officers' territory. There are not many robots near by, but the ones you can see are formidable. One of them signals you. 'Halt! What's the password?' What will you do:

Reply 'Eighty-eight'?	Turn to **120**
Attack immediately?	Turn to **264**
Reply 'Minos'?	Turn to **145**

77

You turn your steps towards the hospital section of the College of Medicine. Soon you find a medikit, which you may add to your Possessions. What will you do now:

Continue to search the hospital?	Turn to **185**
Look for information on sleeping sickness?	Turn to **126**
Leave the hospital?	Turn to **210**

Gary Mayes.

78

You fight the enemy robot. It is a Myrmidon, the standard Karossean combat robot. It has two forms – humanoid and fighter-plane. This one is in humanoid form and will not be able to change itself during the battle.

MYRMIDON

ARMOUR 12 SPEED Medium SKILL 10
SPECIAL ABILITIES: None for this battle

If you reduce the enemy's ARMOUR to 0, turn to **109**. If your own ARMOUR is reduced to 0, turn to **133**.

79

You play for another twenty minutes. When the time ends, the machine goes dark; you will not be able to play it again. But the detailed simulation of combat in the Wasp 200 Fighter has added 1 to your SKILL (with robots only). Return to **288**.

80

'I'm sorry,' replies the Information Robot. 'We have a general medical display in Hall Omicron, but for the kind of specific information you want, you would need to inquire at a hospital, or at the College of Medicine.' If you want to leave the museum, turn to **102**. If you want to ask another question, return to **14** and make another choice.

81

You decide to investigate the Capital City hospital. If you want to stay in your robot, turn to **99**. If you investigate on foot, turn to **152**.

82

The junkyard is just as you left it, but the huge Ape is nowhere in sight. There is nothing that you can do here. Turn to **110**.

83

You fit yourself into the Amplifier Device and activate it. When you take an experimental step, you jump a metre in the air! You reach for the instructions on a nearby table – and your fist goes through the table! You are delighted. You pick up a hundred-kilo file cabinet with one hand, toss it in the air and catch it. Then you try to jump. Maybe you can go over tall buildings with a single bound!

At that point, the suit goes out of control. You bounce off several walls, the floor, and once the ceiling. Eventually you come to a stop. You carefully deactivate the suit – then you just lie and rest. Lose 2 STAMINA points. Now you know why you never heard of this experiment, and why the tester in the sweatsuit looked so battered!

If you leave the building, turn to **206**. If you want to investigate elsewhere, return to **333** and make a new choice.

84

The inquisitive dinosaurs totally surround your quarry. What will you do:

Shove your way in among them?	Turn to **387**
Fire a few shots to panic them?	Turn to **299**
Shout at them over your speakers?	Turn to **119**

85

You are inside the Administrative Building. Everyone is asleep, of course. You see nothing of special interest. What will you do now:

Look for a specific object?	Turn to **17**
Search the whole office thoroughly?	Turn to **96**
Investigate the other building?	Turn to **171**
Get in your robot and cross the electro-fence?	Turn to **129**
Leave the Dinosaur Preserve?	Turn to **150**

86

You summon your courage and confront the Powers of Nothingness. You may not know the meaning of life, but you know you have a mission. And suddenly, nothing feels strange. You stalk out of the Temple of Nothingness. You have gained nothing . . . and lost nothing. Restore the LUCK point that you lost when *Testing your Luck*, and return to **166**.

87

If you are wearing an enemy uniform, turn to **177**. If you do not have a uniform, *Test your Luck*: if you are Lucky, turn to **199**; if you are Unlucky, turn to **223**.

88

'Eighty-eight!' you bark at the Karosseans. 'Seven!' they reply to you. Aha! You have learned the countersign to their password! And because you gave the password, you are free to go about your business. Where were you when you challenged the enemy soldiers:

The City of Industry?	Turn to **132**
The City of Knowledge?	Turn to **63**
The Capital City?	Turn to **192**

89

Your captors discuss what to do with you. Eventually they toss you into a basement room and lock the door. All your Possessions are lost. If you try to escape now, turn to **315**. If you bide your time and wait for a better chance, turn to **397**.

90

Using the Cloak of Invisibility, you easily slip through the enemy lines and into their officers' camp. There you spy Minos himself! If you attack him by surprise, turn to **201**. If you shed your Cloak and try another stratagem, turn to **103**.

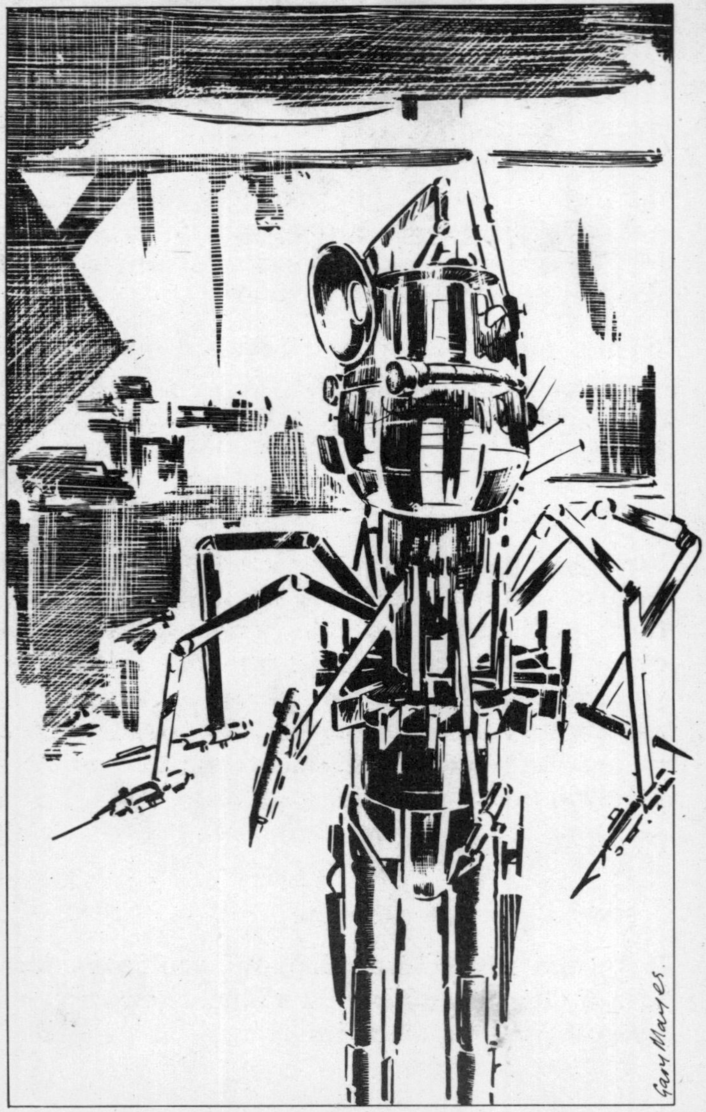

91

Fortunately, the problem seems to be nothing worse than a pair of crossed wires. You activate the robot surgeon and tell it you need treatment. Lights blinking and motors humming, it obliges. Restore all lost STAMINA points and 1 LUCK point. If you now look for information on sleeping sickness, turn to **126**. If you leave the building, turn to **210**.

92

There are no Karosseans left in sight, but you know you had better be off before more appear! Return to **308**.

93

You head for the City of Knowledge. It is your people's greatest centre of learning. There, you hope, you will find information that will help you defeat the invaders. After about an hour of travel, you sight a flying dinosaur ahead of you. It dives aggressively towards you. You must fight it. It is a Pteranodon, a large, predatory flying dinosaur. It is lightly built, but speedy and aggressive.

PTERANODON

ARMOUR 3 SPEED Fast SKILL 9
SPECIAL ABILITIES: None

If you defeat the Pteranodon, or if you *Escape*, turn to **186**. If the Pteranodon reduces your robot's ARMOUR to 0, turn to **116**.

94

The stairway leads to a corridor which turns downward once again. Eventually, the corridor ends in a small alcove with a lift. Rather than retrace your steps, you enter the lift and push the button. Turn to **44**.

95

This is a fatal mistake: you quickly sink into the swampy goo. The dinosaur watches, bemused, as bubbles rise to mark your resting-place.

96

In trying to open an office marked 'Private', you activate a security system. An electric shock pins you to the door-frame. By the time you get free, you have lost 1 STAMINA point. Return to **85**.

97

The battle is over. You have torn the Man-trap Plant into a thousand pieces. Nothing remains of the vicious vegetable except a damper spot on the marshy ground. Turn to **237**.

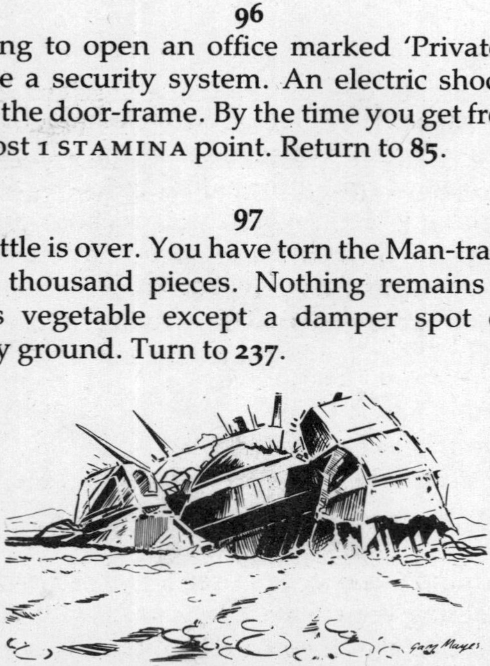

98

You realize that you cannot win a dogfight against this many foes. Dodging and weaving between the buildings of the Capital City, you lose your pursuers. You have stirred up a hornets' nest now! You must press the attack before they hunt you down. What will you do:

Look elsewhere in the Capital City for help? — Turn to **308**

Try to slip into the enemy camp on foot? — Turn to **32**

Stay in your robot and attack on the ground? — Turn to **187**

99

As you round a corner, you see a pair of Karossean robots coming your way! *Test your Luck.* If you are Lucky, turn to **130**. If you are Unlucky, turn to **172**.

100

When your instruments tell you that you have penetrated to the heart of the storm, you take the precious flask of Blue Potion and unstopper it. You quickly pour it through the ejection lock. It diffuses in the air around you. You smile; you know the storm will quickly carry it to every part of Thalos. But when you land, the people of the City of Worship are still asleep. Obviously, the Potion was not sufficiently potent. Turn to **166**.

101

You have defeated the Tylosaurus. Small scavengers are already appearing in the water around you, drawn by the blood. If you return to the city, turn to **144**. If you continue towards the spot where you saw the herd of dinosaurs, turn to **62**.

102

If you possess an Amulet, turn immediately to **250**. Otherwise, you leave the building the way you entered. You re-enter your robot. Turn to **396**.

103

The enemy encampment is well patrolled. You are seized by Karossean guards. If you know something that might help you now, turn to the reference number that came with that information. Otherwise, turn to **228**.

Gary Mayes.

104

Looking at a hospital map, you see that the Research Lab is not far away. Carrying the book with you, you set off to find it, and soon arrive at a large chemical laboratory. As you walked, you heard strange squeaks and shuffling noises in the hallway, but saw nothing. You are somewhat disturbed to note that there are no sleeping doctors or researchers here! No one is here at all.

You bar the lab doors for safety and set to work. Fortunately, the instructions are clear and the lab is well stocked. Eventually, you have a one-litre flask of Blue Potion – all you can make with the materials at hand. Indeed, from the rarity of the materials you used, you doubt that another litre could be made in the whole of Thalos! But you also know from the book that one litre would be enough for everyone in Thalos. Nevertheless, there is a problem. The potion is so volatile that once opened, it will quickly evaporate; you cannot awaken people one at a time. You must find a way to treat your *whole nation* at once! So your quest is not over.

Outside, you hear the strange squeaking once again. If you leave immediately, turn to **394**. If you remain in the laboratory, checking your work one last time, turn to **372**.

105

You decide to visit the Fuel-refining Plant. This is where the radioactive ores that power the robots are processed. A single block of fuel will drive a robot for a year. As you approach, you realize that some of the robots standing around the plant are active! The Karosseans have sent a force to garrison this strategic point. What will you do:

Proceed normally?	Turn to **236**
Attack?	Turn to **169**
Flee?	Turn to **135**
Try a ruse?	Turn to **197**

106

You don the Cloak. It works like a charm: when you walk in front of a store window, you have no reflection! Soon the Cloak is put to a harder test: you walk in front of a Karossean patrol, but remain totally unseen. You enter the Capitol Building itself. There is no sign of the legislators; you assume they have been taken away as hostages. While you are investigating the building, you observe a pair of Karosseans standing guard over a huge display case. You move closer and listen. 'That's right,' one is saying. 'Minos will come to take possession of this sword in a few hours. There'll be some kind of ceremony, I guess.' Looking in the case, you see that this is the Sword of State! You are reluctant to leave it where the tyrant can get it – but taking it would be a risk. What will you do:

Go on and look elsewhere in the Capitol Building? Turn to **164**
Try to take the sword by stealth? Turn to **190**
Attack the sentries and take the sword? Turn to **215**

107

You pray to the Powers of Peace to grant you and your people the peace that can only come from freedom. Somewhere you seem to hear bells chiming, and a feeling of well-being comes over you. Restore your LUCK to its *Initial* score. Return to **166**; you may not visit this temple again.

108

Having provoked a battle, you must now finish it . . . The enemy robot turns and attacks. It is a Battleman, a heavy-duty Karossean combat robot.

BATTLEMAN

ARMOUR 11 SPEED Medium SKILL 11

SPECIAL ABILITIES: If the Battleman's roll exceeds your own roll by 4, it does 1 extra point of damage to you. LUCK rolls will not affect this extra point of damage.

If you defeat the Battleman, turn to **290**. If your own ARMOUR is reduced to 0, turn to **61**. You may not *Escape*.

109

The enemy robot falls, blasted to scrap. There is no sign of its pilot. If you want to examine the fallen robot more carefully, turn to **155**. If you want to ignore it and enter the War College, turn to **65**.

110

You continue to wander about the city for some time. You see many interesting sights, but nothing that looks as though it would help. At length you come to a large open area. At one side of the park is a large building marked 'Robot Experimental Centre'. Across the park is a sign that says 'Robots Working'. It looks like an open access to the city's tunnel system. Will you visit the Robot Experimental Centre (turn to **25**), or leave your robot and enter the tunnel system (turn to **127**)?

111

What will you do:

Challenge Minos to a personal duel?	Turn to **253**
Claim to be a message-bearer?	Turn to **267**
Use a password?	Turn to **173**
Try to fight your way out?	Turn to **283**

112

In the 'Dinosaur Hunt' game, you are given a huge gun with which to fire at holograms representing dinosaurs of all kinds. You fire for a while, but the game is very unrealistic and boring. The dinosaurs seem to walk right past, unaware that they are targets.

You leave in disgust. But, as you do, you notice a plaque by the door. It reads, in part, '. . . this game is based on the prototype "Cloak of Invisibility" device, Model 3, now being tested at the Dinosaur Preserve.' Very interesting! If you want to play another game, turn to **288**. If you would rather leave the arcade, turn to **165**.

113

The enemy robot, trailing smoke, ploughs into the ground. Nothing could have survived that blast. You are free to go. Turn to **63**.

114

You spy an open closet in an adjoining room. Inside you can see a medikit! You investigate; sure enough, the rest of your equipment is here! But as you are gathering it, a rifle-butt strikes your head from behind. Your adventure is over.

115

You hurriedly move to the side. The creature blunders past you and vanishes. You are on the outskirts of the City of the Jungle. If you re-enter the jungle, on the other path, turn to **73**. If you want to go elsewhere, turn to **137**.

116

If you have a flying robot, turn to **139**. Otherwise, turn to **162**.

Gary Mayes.

117

You cross the electro-fence into the Dinosaur Preserve itself. Small lizards scurry about as your robot passes. For several minutes you explore, finding nothing of interest. Then you hear a coughing, trumpeting sound. Charging towards you are two huge, horned Triceratops. Underneath the jungle canopy, shape-changing robots cannot change to flying form; you will have to fight these foes on the ground.

First TRICERATOPS
ARMOUR 9 SPEED Medium SKILL 9
Second TRICERATOPS
ARMOUR 10 SPEED Medium SKILL 8

You must fight them both at once. Each dinosaur will have a separate attack on you in each Attack Round, but you must choose which of the two you will fight. Attack your chosen foe each round as in a normal battle. Against the other you must throw for your Attack Strength in the normal way, but even if your Attack Strength is greater, you will not wound it. You must just count this as though you have defended yourself from it. However, if its Attack Strength is greater, it will damage your robot in the usual way. If you *Escape*, turn to **270**. If you defeat the dinosaurs, turn to **291**. If your robot is destroyed, turn to **310**.

118

You flee down the stairs. If you ever return to this floor, the Guard Robot will still be there, with whatever damage it took during this battle. You find yourself back in the lobby. Turn to **333**.

119

They ignore you totally. Turn to **84** and choose again.

120

'Wrong password, soldier!' comes the response. 'You're in officer territory. Wait! *Stop! That's the Thalian!*' But as the huge sentry robot attacks, you fire also. Turn to **27** and fight.

121

You run, but the Nothosaurus is faster. It gobbles you up in two gulps. Your adventure is over.

122

Your radio suddenly crackles to life with a mechanical voice. 'You are approaching the City of the Guardians. Please give your authorization.' If you have read a military volume on the City of the Guardians, turn to the map reference you were given there. If you have not read this volume, turn to **218**.

123

You enter the temple, but soon find that nothing is what it appears to be. Indeed, nothing is happening here. You seem to have gained nothing by having come. But then, nothing would be served by your leaving! *Test your Luck*. If you are Lucky, turn to **86**. If you are Unlucky, turn to **204**.

124

You make your way to Hall Epsilon. The trip is a long one, and several times you hear odd, echoing sounds. You realize that you are not alone in the building! You press on, and find the exhibition on the history of the Karosseans. Studying it briefly, you see that it has nothing to do with their military abilities; it is all about their culture and customs. It will take an hour to study the material: if you want to do so, turn to **180**. If you return to the front desk, turn to **224**.

125

As your faithful robot disintegrates around you, you hit the 'Eject' button. *Test your Luck.* If you are Lucky, turn to **176**. If you are Unlucky, the ejection system was destroyed in the fight, and your adventure ends here.

126

You follow the signs to the Medical Library. There, amid huge, dusty stacks of books, you begin your search. Finally, in an old textbook, you find a clue to help you. It describes a medicine that – so it says – will instantly cure all types of sleeping sickness. If you will try to compound this medication, turn to **104**. If you would rather leave the hospital, turn to **210**.

127

You park your robot outside the tunnel entrance and slip inside. You don't know what you expect to find here, but you have never been in this tunnel system, and its aura of secrecy attracts you. The tunnels are dimly lit, but you can see well enough. Soon you come to a turning. If you go right, turn to **15**. If you go left, turn to **240**.

128

Soon you arrive at a large clearing. In the middle of the clearing is a huge plant with many spiky leaves. In the centre of the plant, barely within reach, is a stalk bearing several huge red-and-yellow blossoms. What will you do:

Examine the plant more carefully? Turn to **292**
Pick a flower? Turn to **373**
Circle around the plant and continue? Turn to **33**

129

If you fly over the jungle of the Preserve, turn to **252**. If you enter the jungle on the ground, turn to **117**. Note that with some robots, you have a choice between flying or walking!

130

You draw back and freeze your robot into immobility, hugging the corner of a building. Amazingly, they walk right by! You hear a scrap of talk on the radio: '. . . around here somewhere . . .' When they have passed, you proceed to the hospital. Turn to **192**.

131

If you are in the Wasp Fighter, turn to **359**. If you are in any other robot, turn to **378**.

132

Still in your robot, you enter the fuel plant and look around. The building is full of gleaming machinery and stacked canisters of fuel, each worth its weight in gold. But you see nothing that appears likely to help you in your struggle. Furthermore, since your robot was not designed to enter this dangerous environment, you lose 1 STAMINA point because of the radioactivity. Turn to **293**.

133

Test your Luck. If you are Lucky, you manage to guide your crippled robot around the corner before it collapses. Turn to **289**. If you are Unlucky, the last thing you see is the steel fist of the Karossean war machine . . .

134

You try your best to sneak in without being seen – but there are too many enemies about. If you have an enemy uniform and want to wear it for this trip, turn to **243**. If not, turn to **266**.

135

Quickly, you turn your robot. But you were seen. If your robot's speed is Very Fast, turn to **293**. Otherwise, turn to **362**.

136

The enemy fighter swoops around you, its guns hammering. Your canopy cracks. From somewhere behind you, you hear explosions. Then all is darkness. Your adventure is over.

137

You are in the City of the Jungle. If you have been to this city before, turn to **349** immediately. If this is your first visit (no matter how many places you have already been in the city) keep reading.

This is a relatively small city, a home for explorers, gatherers of valuable plants and lovers of the wilderness. Wild dinosaurs often walk the very streets of the City of the Jungle. What will you do here:

Explore the city?	Turn to **366**
Explore the jungle?	Turn to **170**
Leave the city?	Turn to **298**

138

The Ape throws several large chunks of metal at you. Lose 2 ARMOUR points (if this reduces your ARMOUR to 0, turn immediately to **61**). When you attack the Ape, it flees. You look around the junkyard, but the only useful things you see are too heavy for you to move, and the junkyard equipment is out of order. Turn to **110**.

139

Test your Luck. If you are Lucky, you aim your valiant little robot right at the Pteranodon. A second before the crash, you bail out! Lose 1 STAMINA point for cuts and bruises. Your parachute brings you to earth not far from a small village. Turn to 13. If you are Unlucky, you cannot bail out in time. You and your robot spiral together to a fiery doom.

140

When your instruments tell you that you have penetrated to the heart of the storm, you take the precious flask of Lavender Potion and unstopper it. Quickly, you pour it through the ejection lock. It diffuses in the air around you. You smile; you know the storm will quickly carry it to every part of Thalos.

When you land, the people of the City of Worship are already awake. No Karosseans are in sight. Your radio picks up scraps of chatter . . . everywhere, your people are reviving and driving off the Karosean invaders. You have saved your people, and your adventure is over. You are a hero.

141

A claw-like leaf reaches in through a crack in the armour. You scream and strike at it with your sword, but to no avail. A mere human cannot hope to stand against the appetite of the Man-trap Plant! Your adventure is over.

142

Your mission is more important than this asinine robot. You will have to deal with it by force.

GUARD ROBOT	SKILL 8	STAMINA 10

Note that this robot is human-sized, and you fight it as though it were a human foe. You may *Escape* at any time by turning to **118**. If you defeat the Guard Robot, turn to **48**.

Gary Mayes.

143

You enter the National Treasure House. Normally you would never be allowed inside – but now, who is to stop you? You feast your eyes on gold bars of all sizes, sacks of coins and bags of jewels. But you see nothing that looks like a weapon. However, in the warehouse area is a cargo-handling robot. You may take it if you wish. If you have no robot right now, you will certainly take it! This machine looks like a gigantic crab, and is called a Cargo Crab. It has eight legs, plus two huge claws for lifting cargo. Its armoured back opens up to carry heavy loads.

CARGO CRAB

ARMOUR 12 SPEED Slow COMBAT BONUS 0

SPECIAL ABILITIES: The Cargo Crab can carry large quantities of goods or equipment.

If you take the Cargo Crab, you must leave your other robot (if any) at the Treasure House. Now turn to **363**.

144

You are in the City of Storms. This beautiful metropolis is on the sea-coast, and is often the site of spectacular thunderstorms. Where would you like to go:

The Weather Bureau?	Turn to **260**
The coast?	Turn to **335**
Another city?	Turn to **43**

145

The sentry is not fooled. He fires immediately. Lose 2 ARMOUR points and turn to **27**.

146

Hall Beta proves to be a long walk away, through great shadowed corridors. You soon realize that you are lost. Eventually you come to a curtained exhibit-room. The sign over the door reads 'Favours of Fortune'. But inside, you hear strange sounds – like something large moving about. If you enter, turn to **202**. If you go on past, turn to **168**.

147

You are leaving the College of War. Where will you go:

The College of Medicine?	Turn to **54**
The Thalian Museum?	Turn to **14**
The Dinosaur Preserve?	Turn to **66**
Another city?	Turn to **380**

148

Test your Luck. If you are Lucky, turn to **91**. If you are Unlucky, turn to **161**.

149

Suddenly, you find yourself outside the temple. Lose 1 LUCK point for your unwillingness to take chances. Return to **166**; you may not visit this temple again.

150

What would you like to do now:

Visit the College of Medicine?	Turn to **54**
Visit the College of War?	Turn to **277**
Visit the Thalian Museum?	Turn to **14**
Leave the City of Knowledge?	Turn to **380**

151

You feel your robot tipping under you. A marshy spot! Instinctively, you put on a burst of speed to get past the danger. Turn to **237**.

152

You move cautiously through the once busy streets. In the distance you see a pair of enemy robots striding along, but they take no notice of you. You reach the hospital safely. Turn to **192**.

153

You go down a street of tall buildings and turn a corner. In front of you is a Karossean robot! But its back is turned to you. What will you do:

Leave quietly?	Turn to **290**
Attack it?	Turn to **311**
Challenge it?	Turn to **108**

154

Lose 2 STAMINA points. Dazed and bleeding, you are pulled from the wreckage of your robot. 'This is the trouble-maker, all right!' you hear one Karossean say. You do not have time to use medikits right now! If you possess a Karossean uniform, turn to **241**. If not, turn to **89**.

155

You examine the smashed robot. Inside, you see its pilot; he does not appear to be wounded. But as you reach a metal claw towards his bubble, he stabs at a control. His machine self-destructs! Your own robot is thrown back several metres and you are shaken up: lose 2 ARMOUR points and 2 STAMINA points. If your ARMOUR has been reduced to 0, turn to **61**. Otherwise, turn to **65**.

Gary Mayer

156

The ground shakes, and from the shadows comes another enemy war machine to confront you. From within comes a radio transmission: 'Thalian! This is Minos! Now taste *my* wrath!' Your two robots hammer at each other. Around you the Karossean camp is going up in flames. You see a small fighter-robot smashed by a single stray shot. Then you can spare no attention for anything but the battle. The Supertank Minos is piloting is the biggest robot the Karosseans have. It looks like a vast, misshapen tank. A huge gun blazes in front; elsewhere are smaller weapons. Its arms are retracted for safety in the battle.

SUPERTANK

ARMOUR 16 SPEED Slow SKILL 12

SPECIAL ABILITIES: Even on a round in which the Supertank *loses*, you will take 1 point of ARMOUR damage just from its smaller weapons!

If you defeat the Supertank and have some ARMOUR points left for your own robot, turn to **354**. If it reduces your ARMOUR to zero (even if you defeated it at the same time), turn to **6**.

157

The rusty lift clangs shut and begins to ascend. Higher and higher it goes. Then, with a shriek, the cable snaps. The lift descends again, much faster. When it stops, kilometres below the surface, your adventure is over.

158

If you possess the Sword of State, turn to **242**. If you do not possess that sword, turn to **214**.

159

Behind you, your other robot explodes. You dash into the nearest building and down into the cellar. To your surprise, the cellar is very large. In the centre rests a silvery machine with a large corkscrew at the nose. You jump in and close the hatch. The machine starts up. This Borer Robot was designed for travelling under the surface of the earth. It has no weapons or armour, and cannot be used in combat. As you tunnel into the earth, you hear the building collapsing overhead. All the better . . . they will be sure they have killed you. Turn to **338**.

160

As you approach the museum, you see smoke rising from in front of the building. A confused babble of Karossean voices comes over the radio. If you continue, turn to **184**. If you go elsewhere, turn to **63**, but do not choose to return to the museum!

161

You carefully examine the Robot Surgeon. A pair of wires appears to be crossed. But when you switch them, the machine comes alive and grabs you! It seems to want to remove your appendix! Lose 1 STAMINA point immediately! You must fight the berserk machine.

ROBOT SURGEON SKILL 6 STAMINA 8

The room is so small that you cannot *Escape*. If you defeat the Robot Surgeon, turn to **126** to look for information on sleeping sickness, or turn to **210** to leave the building.

162

Your robot crashes to the ground, destroyed. You hide in the wreckage until your assailant goes away. Lose 1 STAMINA point for cuts and bruises. Then you start hiking towards the small village you see on the horizon. Turn to **13**.

163

In the Weather Bureau, you find banks of humming instruments. You also find a printout that explains the flags you saw outside. Apparently a huge storm is due to hit Thalos in a few hours. It will come ashore at the City of Worship, and die away as it rolls over the rest of the land. If you possess a flask of Potion, turn to **213**. If not, turn to **144**.

164

You wander about the Capitol Building until a flickering begins to warn you that the Cloak is running down. Quickly you head back to your robot. Turn to **308**.

165

You are in the City of Pleasure. It is your country's vacation spot, where rich and poor alike come to partake of a thousand different amusements. What would you like to do:

Visit the arcades?	Turn to **288**
Visit the airfield?	Turn to **41**
Leave the city?	Turn to **131**

166

You are in the City of Worship. If you have been to this city before, turn to **67** immediately. If this is your first visit to the city (regardless of how many parts of the city you have been to on this visit), then keep reading.

The whole of this metropolis is devoted to shrines, temples, churches, cemeteries and the like. It is always a quiet place, but you have never before seen it this quiet. Only the call of a sea-bird breaks the stillness. An uneasy thought occurs to you. If you are the only Thalian awake, then the attention of all the Powers must be focused on you personally. Your visit to the City of Worship might be rather . . . interesting. What would you like to do:

Visit one of the temples?	Turn to **49**
Fly over the city (if you have a flying robot)?	Turn to **227**
Go to another city?	Turn to **244**

167

You have chosen a versatile but powerful humanoid robot, a Trouper XI. This is the standard Thalian combat robot. It has two forms: it can shape itself into a giant metal warrior, or into a sleek combat plane.

TROOPER XI

Human Form

ARMOUR 12 SPEED Medium

COMBAT BONUS +2

Plane Form

ARMOUR 10 SPEED Very Fast

COMBAT BONUS +2

SPECIAL ABILITIES: In human form, the Trooper XI carries a gun in one hand and a shield in the other. On an Attack Strength roll of 18 or better, even if the enemy hits it, the robot gets the shield in the way and takes no damage. In plane form, the robot has no special combat abilities.

It takes one combat turn to change forms. During that turn, the robot makes its normal combat roll, but if it wins, it does no damage to the foe – it just defends itself. The shield does *not* protect it on this turn.

You may take one of these robots if you like (there are many here). If you take one and leave, turn to **376**. Or, if you would prefer a tank robot instead, turn to **247**.

168

You continue on your way towards Hall Beta and the military exhibition. When you arrive, it proves to be ancient history. The strange sounds from the building are making you nervous, and you have no desire to read about catapults and other ancient devices. You go back to the main desk. Return to **14**.

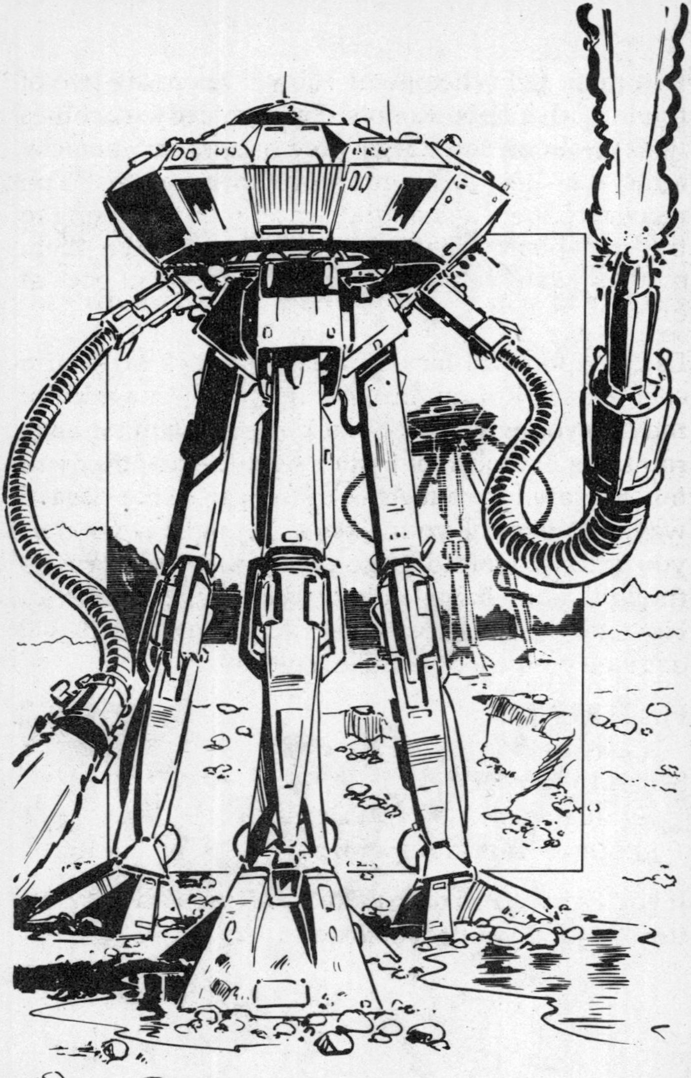

169

You must fight the enemy robots. There are two of them, both Tripod Robots. These speedy machines walk about on three legs; they have metal tentacle-arms that can carry guns or other devices. You recognize them as handling-machines belonging to the fuel plant. The Karosseans have taken them over as guard robots! You must fight them both at once.

Each Tripod will have a separate attack on you in each Attack Round, but you must choose which of the two you will fight. Attack your chosen foe each round as in a normal battle. Against the other you must throw for your Attack Strength in the normal way, but even if your Attack Strength is greater, you will not wound it. You must just count this as though you have defended yourself from it. However, if its Attack Strength is greater, it will damage your robot in the usual way.

First TRIPOD

ARMOUR 7 SPEED Fast SKILL 8

Second TRIPOD

ARMOUR 7 SPEED Fast SKILL 10

SPECIAL ABILITIES: None

If you *Escape*, turn to **293**. If you defeat both Tripods, turn to **30**. If your robot is defeated, turn to **336**.

170

How are you equipped for this trip:

A flying robot? Turn to **285**
A non-flying robot? Turn to **356**
No robot at all? Turn to **64**

171

If you have already opened this building, turn immediately to **231**. Otherwise, keep reading. You walk around the barn-like building and examine it. The walls are built of heavy metal, and the only door you can find is huge. A sign on the door reads, 'DANGER! KEEP OUT!' What will you do:

Open the door? Turn to **212**
Go to the Administrative Building (if you have not already done so)? Turn to **85**
Get in your robot and cross the electro-fence? Turn to **129**
Leave the Dinosaur Preserve? Turn to **150**

172

You're spotted! One of them raises a huge weapon and points it at you. 'What's the password?' it broadcasts. What will you say:

'Seven'? Turn to **262**
'Two-oh-three'? Turn to **203**
'Eighty-eight'? Turn to **88**

173

You give one of the passwords you have learned. But it is of no use. Soon, you are chained to a wall, awaiting the pleasure of Minos. Your adventure is over.

174

You cautiously search through the building. *Test your Luck*. If you are Lucky, turn to **259**. If you are Unlucky, turn to **114**.

175

The computer guides you to the main building of the City of the Guardians. You get out of your robot to investigate. Unfortunately, you soon learn that 'Level Zero' means your security clearance is very low. The Guardian Computer cannot or will not give you full access to the secrets of the base. However, it does seem willing to let you exchange your current robot for a high-powered war robot. (If you do so, make a note of the fact that your old robot remains here.) Will you select a slow, powerful tank robot (turn to **247**), or a speedy shape-changing humanoid/plane robot (turn to **167**)? If you prefer to keep your current robot, turn to **376**.

176

You pop out of the doomed flyer a second before it explodes. The enemy robots shoot past, without seeing you. You feel a tug on your harness – and over you spread the wings of a parasail! You find you can guide it as you please. If you steer for the heart of the enemy encampment, where a crowd of men are looking up at you, turn to **205**. If you steer away and try to lose yourself in the buildings, turn to **226**.

177

Your trick is successful. The enemy pilot sees your uniform and lets you go without asking for the password. He ignores you as you go past him peacefully. Turn to **65**.

178

The tunnel seems to descend for ever. You feel fatigued. Lose 1 STAMINA point. Eventually, it reaches a landing. You take the stairway up: turn to **94**.

179

An hour into your trip, a powerful storm strikes. If your robot is a flying type, turn to **280**. Otherwise, you ride out the storm safely on the ground and then resume your journey: turn to **144**.

180

Just as you are about ready to give up, you stumble across an interesting book on the duelling customs of the Karosseans. Apparently the ancient Karosseans would settle a tribal dispute by choosing champions – one from each tribe – instead of allowing a battle between the whole tribes. The reference number of the book is 111. Make a note of this and turn to **224**.

181

Roll two dice. If the result is less than or equal to your SKILL, turn to **28**. If the result is greater than your SKILL, turn to **318**.

NO ADMITTANCE
Gary Mayes.

182

When you leave the lift on the third floor, you immediately spy a man-sized Guard Robot standing in the hallway. 'Sorry. No admittance,' squawks its mechanical voice. What will you do:

Try to reason with the robot?	Turn to **295**
Attack the robot?	Turn to **142**
Go to another floor?	Turn to **333**

183

You push the 'Eject' button. To your surprise, your cockpit separates and takes off on its own! A second later, the rest of your robot explodes. Seeing the explosion, the Wasp loops away and disappears. You take stock of your new craft: the cockpit of your robot has grown stubby wings and short grasping arms. It is a tiny flying robot, just big enough to hold you – but enough to get you to your destination.

ESCAPE ROBOT

ARMOUR 1 SPEED Very Fast COMBAT BONUS 0

Turn to **137**.

184

You continue towards the museum. When you arrive, you see a strange sight! Two Karossean utility robots are lying wrecked in front of the building. Several Karossean soldiers are also sprawled unmoving. A huge, gleaming, metal Tyrannosaurus is walking in jerky circles in front of the museum. You recognize it as the robot dinosaur that was part of the museum's prize exhibit. The Karosseans must have meddled and activated it!

You are tempted to leave it alone to harass the foe. On the other hand, it is likely to cause damage to the buildings and your sleeping countrymen as well. If you attack the Robot Tyrannosaurus, turn to **207**. If you leave it alone and go elsewhere, turn to **63**, but do not choose to return to the museum!

185

Soon, you spot a sign saying 'SURGERY'. Following it, you see a robot surgeon over a table. But it is marked 'OUT OF ORDER'. If you will try to find what is wrong and repair it, turn to **148**. If you leave it alone and look for information on sleeping sickness, turn to **126**.

186

Not long ago you passed a village. There might be something useful there. If you want to check, turn to **13**. If you want to press on to the City of Knowledge, turn to **361**.

187

You have not gone far before you have to pass through a narrow gate that leads into the outer part of the stadium. There, you are challenged by a group of robots. 'Eighty-eight!' comes the password. If you know the countersign, turn to that number. If not, turn to **50**.

188

Your path narrows; the ground underfoot seems marshy. Roll two dice. If the result is less than or equal to your SKILL for robot control, turn to **151**. If the result is greater than your SKILL, turn to **312**.

189

Everything seems to be as you left it. The Karosseans have no interest in this area, and no desire to get any closer to the monsters than they have to! What will you do:

Leave your robot and go to the Administrative Building?	Turn to **85**
Leave your robot and go to the other building?	Turn to **171**
Stay in your robot and cross the electro-fence?	Turn to **129**
Leave the Dinosaur Preserve?	Turn to **150**

190

Test your Luck. If you are Lucky, you can get behind the case and remove the sword without either guard being the wiser. You hide it under your Cloak and leave the Capitol Building (turn to **296**). If you are Unlucky, one of the guards notices the sword seemingly hanging in mid-air. Turn to **215** and fight.

191

If you had a robot, lose 1 STAMINA point as you are thrown from the wreckage. If you are still alive, you flee on foot as the Nothosaurus demolishes your robot. If you have not already explored the south of the city, you may do so (turn to **225**). Otherwise, you flee into the jungle (turn to **64**).

192

You arrive safely at the Capital City hospital. You can see that you will have to be careful; you hear voices echoing through the halls. If you possess the Cloak of Invisibility and have not used it, you may use it now (turn to **29**). If you have already used it, do not have it, or simply choose not to use it now, turn to **74**.

193

You enter the huge black building. You feel a tremor of uncertainty. As usual, you see sleepers everywhere – but are they really asleep? They look dead! You lift the wrist of the nearest one and check for a pulse. You feel nothing! You look wildly around you, but see nothing. Yet you are terrified . . .

Screaming, you run back outside into the sunlight. When you escape from the temple, the irrational fear vanishes as quickly as it came. But you are still shaking. Reduce your SKILL by 1. If you get hold of yourself and re-enter the grim temple, turn to **327**. Otherwise, return to **166**.

194

The other robot's control bubble springs open, and out flies the Karossean soldier who was piloting it! His unfamiliarity with the controls was fatal: he hit the ejection lever by mistake! He falls under the wheels of his own machine and is lost. If you wish, you can take the Construction Robot instead of your current robot. Its COMBAT BONUS is 0. Whether or not you take it, turn back to **308**.

Gary Mayes.

195

At the outskirts of the city, you find a huge robot junkyard. If you have been here before, turn to **82**. Otherwise, keep reading. As far as the eye can see, scrapped and damaged robots and pieces of robots are standing, sitting and lying on the ground. But out of the corner of your eye, you see motion. Something seems to be watching you from behind a pile of scrap! If you investigate the junkyard, turn to **370**. If you leave, turn to **110**.

196

You soon outdistance the stampeding dinosaurs. You return to the city. Turn to **144**.

197

If you have already been challenged by Karossean soldiers using a number as a password, and you remember that number, turn to that reference. Otherwise, turn to **236**.

198

Just in time, you realize that the lobby is full of Guard Robots like the one you fought before. You quickly return to your robot and leave the area of the Centre. Turn to **206** and make a new choice.

199

Your gamble is successful. The enemy pilot has no reason to believe that any Thalians are awake, so he assumes you must be a friend. He ignores you as you go past him peacefully. Turn to **65**.

200

Because of the practice you got in the arcade game, you know how to handle this robot properly. Turn to **378**.

201

You watch carefully. When your chance comes, you strike! The tyrant falls dead! You attack the other nearby officers. With your Cloak of Invisibility, you are like an avenging demon among them. But there are dozens of them, and they are brave fighters. Eventually, though they can see only your blade, they pull you down by sheer numbers. Your adventure is over. You destroyed the tyrant, but your land is still enslaved. You have failed . . . but it was a glorious failure!

202

To your relief, the sounds you heard were merely the snoring of a very fat man, asleep in a chair. The room is dedicated to exhibits having to do with good and bad luck. You pause to look around. Then your eye is drawn by a display-case at the far end of the room. It must be important – there were two guards beside it! They are still there, fast asleep.

The case contains a jewelled necklace, rather crudely made. But according to the sign on the case, it is a genuine, scientifically proven good-luck charm. This looks as though it might be worth borrowing! You open the case and take the Luck Amulet. Somewhere, you hear an alarm go off, so you hurry away. But the charm is real. Increase your LUCK score (and your *Initial* LUCK) by 1. You go on towards Hall Beta. Turn to **168**.

203

'Wrong, Thalian!' comes the enemy voice. Then both robots attack. Amazingly, one misses! Still, you lose 2 ARMOUR points. Turn to **281**.

204

Why bother, indeed? There seems to be no reason to do anything, and every reason to do nothing. After a while you leave the temple, since nothing is there. When you see the sun again, some of your energy comes back. But you still feel drained. Reduce your STAMINA to 4, if it was higher than 4. Return to **166**.

205

You steer right for the crowd. Amazingly, no one attacks you! You make a creditable landing in the middle of a circle of gaudily uniformed Karosseans. You know that your only chance now is to put on as good a show as possible. If you know something that might help you now, turn to the reference number that came with that information. If not, turn to **228**.

206

You are back in your robot. If you want to explore elsewhere in the City of Industry, return to **265** and pick a new destination. If you want to go to another city, turn to **309**.

207

You decide to fight. The Robot Tyrannosaurus is an intricate device, shaped just like a Tyrannosaurus, but all gears and metal – and tougher than a real dinosaur. It has no pilot, but runs on a pre-set (and very destructive) program.

ROBOT TYRANNOSAURUS

ARMOUR 11 SPEED Fast SKILL 10

If you defeat it, turn to **230**. If it defeats you, turn to **255**. If you *Escape*, turn to **52**.

208

It looks like a gigantic snake! But as you approach, you see it is actually a robot, a Serpent VII. This unit was designed to track and hunt dinosaurs. It has no legs; its gripper-arms fold against the body when not in use. Its shape gives it good mobility in the jungle.

SERPENT VII

ARMOUR 9

SPEED Fast in jungle; Medium elsewhere

COMBAT BONUS +1

SPECIAL ABILITIES: Any time the Serpent's Attack Roll is 16 or better, it can coil around its foe. From then on, it automatically does 1 *extra* point of damage each combat round, regardless of who wins, until it flees or one combatant is destroyed. This does not apply to flying foes.

If you like, you can take the Serpent VII. If you already have a robot, make a note of the fact; that robot will be here should you return. If you have not already explored to the north, you may do so by turning to **16**. Or you may leave off exploring the city and turn to **137**.

209

You set a course for the City of Industry, a place of great factories and machinery. There, you reason, you might find a robot or invention that would give you an advantage over the invaders. If you are in the Dragonfly Robot, turn to **265**. If you are in the Cowboy Robot, turn to **39**.

210

You decide to leave the College of Medicine. You climb back into your trusty robot. Where will you go now:

To the College of War?	Turn to **277**
To the Thalian Museum?	Turn to **14**
To the Dinosaur Preserve?	Turn to **66**
Out of the city?	Turn to **380**

211

You quickly pass the flower in through a port. You unstopper your flask of Potion and drop the flower in. The Potion changes colour to lavender. But, as you put the Lavender Potion safely away, you hear a scratching noise from outside. Turn to **248**.

212

You have a hunch that the barn-like building may contain something of importance. But the door is far too heavy for you to budge. Getting back into your robot, you use its strength to slide open the huge door. Inside you see more robots! Turn to **9**.

213

You realize that this may be just the chance you have been looking for! If you released your Potion into the heart of the storm, it would soon be distributed all over Thalos. But to do this, you will require a flying robot, and you will have to get to the City of Worship. Return to **144**.

214

Minos is a huge, burly man with a curling black beard. His uniform is gold-encrusted and ornate. He studies you with amusement. 'Duel you?' he says. 'Why should I duel you, Thalian vermin?' 'I'm the only Thalian awake!' you reply. 'You *have* to duel me! I demand it!' Around Minos, the other officers mutter. *Test your Luck.* If you are Lucky, turn to **314**. If you are Unlucky, turn to **297**.

215

The guards are not prepared to fight an invisible opponent. Normally crack troops, their SKILL is low for this fight because of their surprise. Fight them one at a time:

First GUARD	SKILL 5	STAMINA 8
Second GUARD	SKILL 4	STAMINA 9

Because of your Cloak, you can *Escape*, if need be, without taking a wound. If you grab the sword and *Escape*, turn to **296**. If you defeat the guards, turn to **334**.

216

Lose 1 LUCK point for cowardice. Return to **308**.

217

Fight them as a single enemy:

MINI-ROBOTS

ARMOUR 9 SPEED Fast SKILL 10

SPECIAL ABILITIES: None

If you *Escape*, turn to **278**. If you defeat the Mini-robots, return to **166** and choose from the options given there. If your ARMOUR is reduced to 0, the Karosseans swarm over you, and your adventure ends here.

218

You realize that you have stumbled on to a top-secret military base. Frantically, you tell the computer what has happened. *Test your Luck.* If you are Lucky, turn to **337**. If you are Unlucky, turn to **2**.

219

If you are wearing a Karossean uniform, turn to **303**. If not, turn to **11**.

220

Since your robot is not designed for cargo, you can carry only a small amount of gold. If you want to load up what you can, turn to **287**. If you leave empty-handed, turn to **308**.

Gary Mayes.

221

You sit down in the seat. Instantly, you find yourself at the controls of a sleek fighter – the experimental Wasp 200! For twenty minutes you seem to fly through the skies, pursuing enemy robots. Then a timer buzzes and you find yourself back at the Arcade. In front of you, a screen is blinking 'Advanced Game Ready!' You have earned extra time. If you decide to play the extra time, turn to **324**. If you leave this game, turn to **288**.

222

'Pass, friend!' the sentry robot transmits. 'But don't go past the next ring. That's officer country.' If you continue in your robot, turn to **76**. If you enter on foot, turn to **32**.

223

From within his robot, the Karossean sentry challenges you. Your reply does not satisfy him. You must fight! Turn to **78**.

224

You leave the military display and take a short cut through a hallway overlooking a huge gallery. As you look down, you are surprised to see devastation! A huge area of exhibits has been demolished. Two black-clad Karossean soldiers are lying there, dead or wounded, and a trail of devastation leads right through a huge hole in the wall. You hear shouts from below. If you would like to go down and investigate, turn to **374**. If you would rather avoid the area and head back towards the information desk, return to **14**.

225

You go south through the deserted city. Small lizards scuttle about. You remember that you are not far from the edge of the jungle here. Ahead you see a long, gleaming shape, like a huge length of mottled pipe. What will you do:

Investigate it?	Turn to **208**
Turn around and search the north (if you have not done so already)?	Turn to **16**
Abandon your city exploration?	Turn to **137**

226

You steer towards an area of wooded parkland, hoping to escape. But they are tracking you. When you land, you are surrounded almost before you can remove your harness, and taken off to prison. A good try – but not good enough. Your adventure is over.

227

A violent storm is coming from over the ocean; it will strike land in minutes. If you fly into the storm, turn to **12**. If you fly inland, away from the storm and the city, turn to **244**.

228

If you try to bluff your way out of this situation, turn to **267**. If you try to fight your way past, turn to **283**.

229

On the tenth floor, you find an incredible confusion of cubbyholes, and nothing that looks like a robot or device. There are tall bookshelves everywhere, and more books on the floor and the desks. If you continue to investigate, turn to **360**. If you return to the lobby, turn to **333**.

230

You have defeated your strange foe. It falls, a smoking wreck. Regain 2 LUCK points for defending your people from this unusual menace. You know the battle will soon draw Karossean attention, and you had better not come back here. You leave; you may not return to the museum again. Turn to **63**.

231

The barn-like building where you found the robots is also as you left it. Your old robot is there – you may take it back if you like. Or you may get another Super-Cowboy Robot. What will you do now:

Walk over to the Administrative Building? — Turn to **85**
Get in your robot and cross the electro-fence? — Turn to **129**
Leave the Dinosaur Preserve? — Turn to **150**

232

As you walk down the corridors of the hospital, you hear a strange squeaking and rustling noise coming from all around you. You see by the signs that you are in the Research Lab section. The noise does not sound human – but it is certainly no robot! You feel better with your sword in hand.

You step through a pair of double doors, into a room full of large wire cages. You see that some are opened. Then you realize what the sounds were. The hospital's experimental animals have escaped . . . and they are hungry!

You turn to run, but your way is blocked. You are facing three Giant Lizards! Backing into the corner of the room, you may fight them one at a time, in order. You cannot try to *Escape* until you have slain the first two.

	SKILL	STAMINA
First GIANT LIZARD	7	4
Second GIANT LIZARD	6	6
Third GIANT LIZARD	7	5

If you defeat all three Giant Lizards, or if you successfully *Escape*, turn to **254**.

233

If your robot is a humanoid type, turn to **351**. Otherwise, turn to **318**.

Gary Mayes.

234

You speak calmly to the Ape, and it begins to caper and grunt. It is a pet, kept to help around the yard! You look around the junkyard, but the only useful things you see are too heavy for you to move, and the junkyard equipment is out of order. Then the Ape, which has been watching you, lends a hand. Deftly, it takes apart the robot you have been studying, and carries the parts as you indicate. With the help of the Ape, you may repair up to 4 ARMOUR points on your robot, if that many had been lost. Turn to **110**.

235

Your robot is scratched and dented, but you have won. Lose 1 STAMINA point for the bruises you took when the monster knocked your robot over. You continue on your way towards the City of Industry. Turn to **265**.

236

Over the radio comes a challenge: 'Eighty-eight!' If you know the countersign that is required for that password, turn to the number of the countersign. If you do not know the proper response, turn to **389**.

237

You continue through the jungle. It is hard going; hidden pits and logs take their toll on your robot. Reduce its ARMOUR by 2. (If this reduces its ARMOUR to 0 or less, leave its ARMOUR at 1.) Eventually, the city comes into view; you are relieved! But, as you enter it, you twice see flying Karossean robots patrolling overhead. Each time you hold your own robot motionless and they overlook you. But you realize that this city is no longer safe; there are Karosseans everywhere. If you came to this city in another robot and you would like to switch back to it, turn to **45**. If you stay in your current robot to leave the city, turn to **298**.

238

You eject from the battered robot and run for your life. *Test your Luck.* If you are Lucky, you evade pursuit: return to **308** (without your robot!). If you are Unlucky, your adventure ends here in capture and defeat.

239

You attack the Iguanodon that is blocking your way. This plant-eating dinosaur walks on two legs. It is tough and heavy-set, and its spiky 'thumbs' are good weapons.

IGUANODON

ARMOUR 5 SPEED Medium SKILL 9

You cannot *Escape*. If you defeat the Iguanodon, turn to **137**. If your robot's ARMOUR is reduced to 0, turn to **306**.

240

The tunnel winds until you have lost all sense of direction. Then it forks. One fork seems to go up; the other turns downward. If you go up, turn to **72**. If you go down, turn to **15**.

241

Your captors do not even discuss what to do with you; they stand you against a wall and shoot you as a spy. Your adventure is over.

242

Minos is a huge, burly man with a curling black beard. His uniform is gold-encrusted and ornate. He studies you with amusement. 'Duel you?' he says. 'Why should I duel *you*, Thalian vermin?' 'I'm the only Thalian awake!' you reply. 'And I have the Sword of State! That makes me the representative of all Thalos! You *have* to duel me!'

Around Minos, the other officers mutter. 'He's right,' says one. 'It's the law,' you hear another say. Others agree with them. Minos frowns angrily. Then he laughs. 'Very well, since you insist!' he says. 'We will fight. Right now!' The Sword of State is returned to you. You may now fight Minos himself! Turn to **330**.

243

With the uniform, you try to bluff your way in. But soon a beribboned officer calls to you, 'Sergeant! Over here!' You have no hope of bluffing it out. You dash around a corner, rip the uniform off and keep running. By the time a patrol rounds the corner, you are across the street, feigning sleep. But you will not be able to enter the Capitol Building. Lose 1 point of STAMINA. You return to your robot. Turn to **308**.

244

You are leaving the City of Worship. Where would you like to go:

The Capital City?	Turn to **308**
The City of Knowledge?	Turn to **361**
The City of Storms?	Turn to **144**

245

You are blasted out of the sky. Your adventure ends here.

246

As you jet through the water, you see a huge shadow swimming to intercept you. It is a Tylosaurus, one of the most feared of marine dinosaurs. This monster looks like a cross between a huge, toothy lizard and a shark; it has finny paddles instead of legs. It normally lives on fish, but is willing to try a robot for variety!

TYLOSAURUS

ARMOUR 9	SPEED Medium	SKILL 10

Note that, in the water, your robot's speed is also Medium, so neither of you has a disadvantage. If you lose this battle, you will be drowned or eaten, if not both. If you win, turn to **101**.

247

You have chosen a powerful Robotank. This fearsome war machine looks like a human from the waist up. From the waist down, it is a huge tank, with terrible twin guns. It is one of the few 'battle-line' machines your land possesses.

ROBOTANK

ARMOUR 18 SPEED Slow

COMBAT BONUS +2

SPECIAL ABILITIES: The Robotank contains a special Sonic Gun in one hand. It cannot be used by any other robot. It may be fired once per combat turn, in addition to the Robotank's regular attack. However, it may be used only three times in all; then it is useless. When fired, the Sonic Gun is instantly deadly to unprotected humans. Against a robot, roll one die to see how many ARMOUR points the target loses. Against a dinosaur, roll two dice to see how many ARMOUR points the target loses.

There are three of these robots here. You may take one and leave (turn to **376**), or, if you prefer, you may turn to **167** to take a faster robot.

248

The spiky leaves reach towards you, and the flower stalk pulls back to show a fanged mouth. The plant is hungry!

MAN-TRAP PLANT

ARMOUR 8	SPEED see below	SKILL 9

Since the Man-trap Plant has caught hold of you before the battle starts, differences in Speed do not matter. You cannot *Escape*. If you defeat the Man-trap Plant, turn to **97**. If it reduces your ARMOUR to 0, turn to **141**.

249

You decide to visit the Temple of Nothingness. You have never been there before, and you have no idea what to expect. When you arrive, you see the usual sprawled forms on the sidewalk in front. Several were carrying signs and placards. Were they protestors? You look at a sign; it reads, 'Nothing is wrong.' If you would rather not get involved with this strange bit of business, you may return to **166**. If you want to go inside, turn to **123**.

250

You wave to the robot and start to leave . . . but as you do, alarms go off and lights flash. 'I'm very sorry,' says the robot, 'but museum property has been removed without authorization. You cannot leave.' Its metal arms reach out towards you. Roll two dice. If the number you roll is less than or equal to your SKILL, turn to **272**. Otherwise, turn to **294**.

251

You have returned to the Robot Experimental Centre. If you acquired the Seeker Missile on a previous visit, turn to **198**. If not, turn to **333**.

252

You soar over the jungle of the Dinosaur Preserve, but see nothing of interest. You don't know what you expected to find out here, anyway! You decide to leave. Turn to **150**.

253

You demand the right, as a representative of your people, to duel Minos. The officer in charge shakes his head. 'Search him!' he orders his men. Your heart sinks. You are stripped of all your Possessions (including medikits). But then the sentries take you directly to Minos himself. Turn to **158**.

254

Near by you hear more squeaking and shuffling. There were many more than three opened cages in the lab. If you search through the lab, turn to **276**. If you leave the College of Medicine, turn to **210**.

255

Your robot falls, torn by the shining steel teeth of the mechanical enemy. Lose 2 STAMINA points. As soon as your robot stops moving, your foe loses interest and goes tramping away. When it is gone, you investigate your surroundings. You find that one of the wrecked Karossean robots is still just usable. You get in and check it out. It is a general-purpose Karossean robot, humanoid in shape. It has been badly battered, so your COMBAT BONUS is *negative* while you are in it.

UTILITY ROBOT

ARMOUR 4 SPEED Slow COMBAT BONUS −2
SPECIAL ABILITIES: None

Your only thought is to get away as quickly as possible. You know that your unsuccessful battle will soon draw Karossean attention, and you had better not come back here. You leave; you may not return to the museum again. Turn to **63**.

256

The book gives you the location of the City of the Guardians, the secret base that is the headquarters of the army of Thalos. The map reference is **22**. Make a note of this number. Substitute it for 'XX' when you are given the option to visit the City of the Guardians. You may find another use for the map reference, as well. For now, of course, you must deal with the Karosseans outside the building you are in! Turn to **368**.

257

You try the advanced game . . . but it is far too hard for you. Over and over you are shot down. When your time is up, you emerge, shaking. That machine was too realistic! Lose 1 point of STAMINA. Return to **288**.

258

The dinosaur is not satisfied with its victory. Ripping and tearing, it demolishes your robot completely. It knows that the robot isn't good to eat, but it smells meat somewhere! *Test your Luck.* If you are Lucky, turn to **282**. If you are Unlucky, turn to **391**.

259

You spy an open closet in an adjoining room. Inside you can see a medikit! You investigate; sure enough, the rest of your Possessions are here! You hastily collect them all and escape through a convenient window. Turn to **69**.

Gary Mayes.

260

Flying over the Weather Bureau are the two red flags that you know mean 'STORM WARNING!' Parked outside the building you see another robot, a Walker Robot. Designed primarily for travel, this robot has four jointed legs that carry it swiftly over any terrain.

WALKER ROBOT

ARMOUR 6 SPEED Fast COMBAT BONUS −1
SPECIAL ABILITIES: None

If you like, you may exchange this robot for your own. If you come back to this spot after exchanging, your own robot may still be here; make a note that this is where you are leaving it. If you go inside the Weather Bureau, turn to **163**. If you go on past, turn to **144**.

261

You turn aside and leave your own robot in order to examine this one. It is low-slung and seems spiky. You see that it is bristling with weapons, which is what gives the Hedgehog Robot its name. It was designed for air defence against flying dinosaurs, but it is equally effective against flying robots.

HEDGEHOG ROBOT

ARMOUR 8 SPEED Slow
COMBAT BONUS 0 or +3
SPECIAL ABILITIES: Against flying foes, the Hedgehog has a COMBAT BONUS of +3, which more than cancels out its disadvantage in speed.

If you like, you may exchange your present robot for this one. If you do so, make a note that your old robot is now parked here instead of the Hedgehog. If you go on towards the Temple of Fear, turn to **57**. If you return the way you came, turn to **166**.

262

There is a brief buzz of conversation between your enemies. Your answer seems to have confused them. If you decide to attack immediately, turn to **281**. If you stand your ground without attacking, turn to **203**.

263

It is a large Crawler Robot. The crew, of course, is asleep, and you do not want to take their robot and leave them to the jungle. But within the robot is an interesting piece of equipment, like nothing you have ever seen. Reading the Crawler pilot's orders, you see the following: '. . . experimental Tangler Field works on flying machines – but not always. Your orders are to test it against flying dinosaurs immediately.' Beneath this is written, in large red letters, 'NO GOOD!'

You may add the Tangler Field to your Possessions and continue. If you explore the other path of the jungle, turn to **73**. If you want to go elsewhere, turn to **137**.

264

Your attack catches the enemy by surprise. Turn to **27**, but you automatically win the first combat round without rolling!

265

You are in the City of Industry. Normally, it is busy and bustling, but now you see no life anywhere. Everyone is asleep . . . everyone but you. Where will you go in your quest for useful artefacts:

The Fuel-refining Plant?	Turn to **105**
The Robot Experimental Centre?	Turn to **25**
The tunnels underneath the city?	Turn to **127**
Just explore?	Turn to **34**
Leave the city?	Turn to **309**

266

The building is crawling with Karosseans. There is no point in even thinking about entering. You return to your robot. Turn to **308**.

267

'I've got an important message for Minos himself!' you shout. 'You've got to let me through!' But your bluff does not work. They drag you away and throw you into the slave-pits. Your adventure is over.

268

It is a complete book of instructions on handling all types of enemy combat robots! You laugh, thinking of the surprise you can now give the Karosseans, if you get the chance. Turn to 368.

269

Which button will you press:

Green?	Turn to 369
Red?	Turn to 157
Blue?	Turn to 44

270

You are shaken up; lose 1 STAMINA point. Because of the narrow jungle trails, your robot takes 3 points of damage as it escapes. If this is enough to bring its ARMOUR to 0, turn to **310**. Otherwise, you flee the jungle: turn to **189**.

271

Well, this is war. You circle behind the hapless sentry – then rush him. Your sword swings silently and he is dead. Turn to **143**.

272

You dodge underneath the mechanical arms with which it is trying to stop you, and through the door. You quickly climb into the control seat of your robot. Turn to **396**.

Gary Mayes.

273

You find nothing else of interest in the shop. As you leave, the hammering noise continues behind you. The repair shop is awake, even if its masters are asleep. Turn to **110**.

274

If you are flying, turn to **341**. If you are travelling on the ground, turn to **5**.

275

Your battle has caused great confusion. Stray shots are wreaking havoc among the Karosseans and their lesser robots. But now a group of sleek fighter-craft swoop out of the sky to challenge you. If you have the Tangler Field and wish to activate it, turn to **301**. If you do not have this device (or do not wish to use it), turn to **326**.

276

This is a fatal error. Minutes later, you are trapped in a dead-end corridor by dozens of hunger-maddened laboratory animals, many of which are mutations – a most embarrassing end for a hero . . .

277

The College of War is easy to find; it is a huge five-sided building built all of brick. If you have been here before, turn to **332**. If you have not been here before, keep reading. A robot of unfamiliar design is standing in front of the building. You recognize it as a Karossean military robot. What will you do:

Attack immediately?	Turn to **46**
Try to pass as one of the invaders?	Turn to **87**
Leave before you are noticed?	Turn to **147**

278

What will you do now:

Fly into the storm (if you have a flying robot)?	Turn to **12**
Leave the city, travelling on the ground?	Turn to **244**
Explore the temples?	Turn to **49**

279

Test your Luck. If you are Lucky, turn to **191**. If you are Unlucky, turn to **121**.

280

Roll one die. If you roll 1 or 2, turn to **122**. If you roll 3, 4, 5 or 6, turn to **144**.

281

Fight the two enemy Myrmidon robots, one at a time. The Myrmidon is the standard Karossean combat robot. It has two forms – humanoid and fighter-plane. These are in humanoid form and will not try to change during the battle.

First MYRMIDON
ARMOUR 11 SPEED Medium SKILL 10
Second MYRMIDON
ARMOUR 12 SPEED Medium SKILL 9
SPECIAL ABILITIES: None in this combat

If you defeat the two robots, turn to **192**. If they reduce your robot's ARMOUR to 0, turn to **238**. If you *Escape*, turn to **308**.

282

While the Tyrannosaurus is tearing up the robot's torso, you dodge out of the cockpit, grab your backpack with your supplies and run into the shelter of the boulders. Lose 3 STAMINA points for your injuries. You carefully depart, and gradually the sounds of roaring and destruction fade into the distance. Turn to **367**.

283

You fight bravely, but there is no way you could possibly prevail against such numbers. Though you take several invaders with you, you are slain.

284

Flying over the sea-coast, you see nothing of interest except a huge herd of dinosaurs. They are clustered around something, but you cannot make out what it is. If you return to the city, turn to **144** and make another choice. If your robot can change shape to a land-going form, you may land and investigate the sea-coast: turn to **8**.

285

You realize that a flying robot is the wrong type for jungle exploration. What will you do:

Transform your robot into a walking shape (if you can) and enter the jungle?	Turn to **356**
Leave the city?	Turn to **298**
Explore the city?	Turn to **366**

Gary Mayes.

286

'Then face your foe!' comes the answer. In front of you appears a Karossean soldier, armed like yourself. You must fight him.

SOLDIER SKILL 10 STAMINA 10

If you *Escape*, turn to **21**. If you defeat him, turn to **352**.

287

In the middle of your labour, you hear a grinding noise – and look up to see three huge tanks and a dozen grinning soldiers. Resistance would be useless. And, to add insult to injury, they do not treat you as a prisoner of war, but a common criminal. You are sent to a life of hard labour in the Karossean slave-pits. Your adventure is over – and it was not a heroic ending.

288

You are in the Arcade building, with your robot parked outside. It is a madhouse of sound and coloured lights. Each arcade game is wilder than the next. Which one will you play:

Wasp Fighter?	Turn to **221**
Dinosaur Hunt?	Turn to **112**
Zap the Karossean?	Turn to **393**
None of these?	Turn to **165**

289

As your robot falls, you pop out of the hatch and roll safely away. You crawl under a bush near the wall and wait. The great steel foot of the enemy robot lands close to your head as it charges in pursuit. But it merely puts a few more shots into your wrecked robot and continues past, without seeing you. As you lie in hiding, you hear other robots arrive, as well as troopers on foot. But they seem to be looking for an invading force, rather than a single fugitive. Eventually, most of them go inside the building – leaving one of their war robots standing empty, a stone's throw from your hiding-place! If you make a dash for the robot, turn to **345**. If you stay in hiding, turn to **61**.

290

You clank through a small park and down a short street. In front of you, you see a crowd of Karossean soldiers, looting a shop. If you turn and flee, turn to **216**. If you fight them, turn to **343**.

291

You have defeated both the Triceratops. Lose 1 STAMINA point due to the stress of the fight with the great horned dinosaurs. You realize that entering this area was a mistake; you will find nothing here but more danger! You quickly retrace your steps. Turn to **189**.

292

As you examine the plant, you get the uneasy feeling that it is examining *you* too. Turn to **248**.

293

At your best speed, you leave the area of the Fuel-refining Plant. You may not return to this site. Turn to **265**.

294

The robot catches you. You must fight it as though it were a human opponent; this is a small robot, not a monster like the ones you have piloted, so your sharp sword may be enough to deal with its spindly arms!

INFORMATION ROBOT	SKILL 6	STAMINA 10

If the robot reduces your STAMINA to 2, turn to **344**. If you defeat the robot, turn to **320**.

295

While you are arguing with the machine, it picks you up – none too gently – and tosses you back into the lift. Lose 1 STAMINA point. If you leave the floor, turn to **333** and make a new selection. If you attack the robot, turn to **142**.

296

You escape easily. The guards have no idea what has happened. You have captured the Sword of State – a large, ornate blade. To your surprise, it is sharp and well balanced. When you use it to fight a foe, increase your SKILL by 1. Turn to **358**.

297

The tyrant shakes his head. 'Just because you're a Thalian doesn't mean I have to duel you. Take him away!' You have done your best, but it wasn't enough. Your adventure is over.

298

You are leaving the City of the Jungle. Where will you go:

The City of Industry?	Turn to **265**
The City of Knowledge?	Turn to **361**
The City of Pleasure?	Turn to **165**
The Capital City?	Turn to **308**

299

You aim your weapons over their heads and fire a few times, hoping to herd them away from you. This is a mistake! They panic and run in all directions – and the narrow beach funnels many of them right at you. You are in the path of several hundred tonnes of frightened dinosaur! What will you do:

Take off (if your robot can also fly)?	Turn to **181**
Try to outrun them?	Turn to **371**
Head for the water?	Turn to **233**

300

It proves to be a useless volume of obscure military regulations. You cast it aside in irritation, but you have no time to examine another book. Turn to **368**.

301

You quickly activate the Tangler Field. The attacking flyers veer wildly. Two collide; several others crash into the ground. The survivors streak away in panic, and the sky is clear. Turn to **156**.

302

As you leave the research labs, you hear once again the strange shuffling and squeaking. You step through a pair of double doors, into a room full of large wire cages. You see that some are opened. Then you realize what the sounds were. The hospital's experimental animals have escaped . . . and they are hungry! You are facing a trio of red-eyed Giant Lizards. If you fight the creatures, turn to **328**. If you turn to flee, turn to **350**.

303

You round a corner – and run right into three Karossean doctors! They look at you keenly. What will you do:

Pretend to faint?	Turn to **323**
Attack them?	Turn to **353**
Apologize and go on your way?	Turn to **375**

304

You decide to visit the Temple of Fear. On your way there, you see an unusual robot parked in an open space. If you stop to investigate it, turn to **261**. If you go straight to the temple, turn to **57**.

305

Over the radio, the Karossean challenges you: 'Eighty-eight!' If you know the proper countersign for a response, turn to that number. If not, you will have to fight: turn to **26**.

306

You bound out of the wrecked robot and into the swamp, where the beast cannot follow. Turn to **95**.

307

The lift shoots quickly upward. The force of its acceleration almost knocks you down – and it continues for a long time! Suddenly the lift doors pop open. You are in the lobby of the Robot Experimental Centre. If you cross the square and re-enter your robot, turn to **206**. If you investigate the Robot Experimental Centre, turn to **25**.

308

You are in the Capital City – the seat of government of Thalos. It is a noble city, full of white marble buildings. It is also the main base of the invaders, and you know you must be very careful!

Below, you have five options. Some of them will eventually return you to this paragraph. You may not make the same choice twice; each time you return here you must make a new selection. Where will you go:

The city hospital?	Turn to **81**
The Capitol Building?	Turn to **10**
The National Treasure House?	Turn to **385**
The enemy encampment?	Turn to **4**
Just explore?	Turn to **31**

309

You are leaving the City of Industry. Where will you go now:

The City of Knowledge?	Turn to **361**
The City of Pleasure?	Turn to **165**
The City of the Jungle?	Turn to **38**
The City of the Guardians?	Turn to **1XX**

Note that you may not go to the City of the Guardians unless you have learned the way and know the numbers to substitute for the 'XX'.

310

Trapped in the Dinosaur Preserve, without a robot to carry you, you have little hope. *Test your Luck* twice in succession. If you are Lucky both times, turn to **329**. Otherwise, turn to **348**.

311

Test your Luck. If you are Lucky, turn to **325**. If you are Unlucky, turn to **108**.

312

You feel your robot tipping under you. A marshy spot! Instinctively, you put your machine in reverse. Too slow . . . You sink slowly into the marsh. You try to fire your ejection seat, but it fails to function. You are doomed to a lingering death in the muck.

313

Roll one die. On a roll of 1, 2 or 3, turn to **137**. On a roll of 4, 5 or 6, turn to **341**.

314

The tyrant shakes his head. 'Just because you're a Thalian doesn't mean I have to duel you.' But, hearing his men grumble, he adds: 'Until you prove yourself, that is. If you can defeat one of my officers, that will prove you are worthy to face me.' Instantly, one of his followers – a big, scarred brute – leaps out with drawn sword. Your sword is returned to you. You will have to fight the Karossean officer.

OFFICER	SKILL 11	STAMINA 11

If you win, turn to **377**.

315

You smash several pieces of furniture against the door, but to no avail. Your prison seems solid. Lose 1 STAMINA point. Turn to **397**.

316

You regain control of your flyer, though the buffeting is terrible. Lose 1 STAMINA point. If you have a flask of liquid in your possession, count the letters in both words of its name, multiply that number by 10, and turn to that reference. If you have no flask, turn to **166**.

317

You step cautiously inside, ready to fight if need be. But the sounds were being made by an automated repair facility, hard at work stamping out armour-plate. There is no sign of anyone awake. You leave your robot and investigate the controls of the repair shop. They seem simple enough. If you would like to attempt repairs on your robot, turn to **59**. If your robot needs no repairs, or if you do not choose to attempt repairs, turn to **273**.

318

Unfortunately, your attempt fails. You are too slow to get out of the way. No matter how big your robot, the terrified beasts are bigger. Your adventure ends here, as you and your machine are both crushed into tin foil by a rampaging herd of dinosaurs.

319

This is almost too easy! You proceed past the sentry as though everything were all right – then, at the last second, you change course. The last thing the sentry sees is the huge hulk of your machine looming over him. Turn to **143**.

320

One by one, you chop off the robot's arms. At last it is helpless. You feel a bit sorry as you run out of the door; the robot was only doing its duty. As you leave, it is still hooting mournfully, 'Return the museum's property, please!' You quickly climb into the control seat of your robot. Turn to **396**.

321

If you explore the jungle on the other path, turn to **73**. If you want to go elsewhere, turn to **137**.

322

You reach for the controls. The enemy pilots are still not in sight. If you want to try to destroy the other robots, turn to **381**. If you just want to leave, turn to **399**.

323

The doctors pick you up and hoist you between them to a treatment room. Soon a robot surgeon is working on you. Restore your STAMINA to its *Initial* level. As soon as you are left alone in a recovery room, you take your leave. Unfortunately, your uniform is gone. You borrow suitable clothes from a sleeping man in the hallway and continue. If you look for information on sleeping sickness, turn to **395**. If you leave the hospital and return to your robot, turn to **308**.

324

Test your Luck. If you are Lucky, turn to **79**. If you are Unlucky, turn to **257**.

Gary Mayes.

325

The enemy robot's control bubble explodes in a cloud of greasy black smoke. Small fragments clatter and ring off the pavement and your own armour. The headless body stands for a moment, then collapses in a pile of junk! One Karossean down, a thousand to go. Turn to **290**.

326

There are far too many of them to fight. The area is littered with smoking wreckage before you are through. You have dealt a severe blow to the invaders, but you did not defeat them. Your adventure is over.

327

You grit your teeth and summon up your courage – and go back inside. But it is worse than before. The Powers of Fear are all around you. Whatever help they may be able to give, you want none of it! Lose another SKILL point and return to **166**.

328

You are facing three Giant Lizards! You back into the corner of the room, so that you may fight them one at a time. You cannot try to *Escape* until you have slain the first two.

	SKILL	STAMINA
First GIANT LIZARD	7	4
Second GIANT LIZARD	6	6
Third GIANT LIZARD	7	5

If you defeat all three, or if you successfully *Escape*, turn to **254**.

329

Torn and bleeding after several encounters with small dinosaurs, you stagger out of the Dinosaur Preserve. Lose 3 STAMINA points, one at a time (so, if you have medikits, you can cure each one as it is lost). If you have already investigated the unmarked building, turn to **364**. If you have not investigated that building, turn to **383**.

330

Minos draws a huge, jewelled sword. You know he did not become Tyrant of Karossea by being soft or weak. But you didn't get this far by being weak, either. 'Defend yourself, Karossean!' you shout. A murmur – could it be approval? – rises from the watching officers. You battle Minos – to the death!

MINOS	SKILL 12	STAMINA 12

If you win, turn to **355**.

331

You flee from the Nothosaurus. If you are in a robot, turn to **382**. If you are on foot, turn to **279**.

332

As you approach the War College, you see two Karossean robots guarding it, and black-clad foot soldiers milling about. Fortunately, you were cautious in your approach, and they have not seen you. There can be nothing here worth entering that hornets' nest for! You quickly change course. Turn to **147**.

333

You are in the lobby of the Robot Experimental Centre. You read the directory, and see that different sorts of work are being done on different floors of the building. Several seem interesting. Where will you go:

Second floor: Interface Mechanisms? Turn to **392**
Third floor: Weapons Development? Turn to **182**
Sixth floor: Amplifier Project? Turn to **20**
Tenth floor: Deteronics? Turn to **229**
Leave the building? Turn to **206**

334

You have defeated the guards. Other soldiers are running from all directions, but they cannot see you. You have captured the Sword of State, a large, ornate blade. To your surprise, it is sharp and well balanced. When you use it to fight a foe, increase your SKILL by 1. Turn to **358**.

335

You pilot your robot along the sea-coast. If you are flying, turn to **284**. If you are not flying, turn to **8**.

336

Your robot falls and you lie stunned in the wreckage. The tentacles of a Tripod pull you out. You are a prisoner of the Karosseans! You have failed in your mission. Your adventure is over.

337

'Correct,' replies the computer. 'All Thalian personnel have been disabled by Karossean attack using Sudden Sleeping Sickness. My sensors show no other citizen of Thalos still awake. You are granted base entry at Level Zero.' Turn to **175**.

Gary Mayes.

338

You have no control over the Borer Robot's path. For hours it tunnels underground; then it turns upward again. Eventually it reaches the surface, and you open the hatch into daylight. You seem to be in a small town. You will need to find new transportation; the Borer Robot will not stir from its new site.

The only robot you can find to take you there, unfortunately, is an ancient, rattling Stilter. This is a very tall, thin robot, apparently designed for painting the upper storeys of buildings or something of the sort. Its arms and legs are very long. You hope this tired, creaky machine will make the trip safely.

STILTER

ARMOUR 4 SPEED Medium
COMBAT BONUS −1
SPECIAL ABILITIES: None

You are midway between two cities. If you will go to the City of Knowledge, turn to **361**. If you will go to the City of Worship, turn to **166**.

339

You decide to visit the Temple of Glory. After all, glory is what you will earn if you can drive off the Karosseans! The temple is large and stately, with multicoloured mosaics of battle scenes on the outer walls. You enter and approach the altar. You feel the presence of the Powers of Glory very strongly. A voice seems to ring in your head: 'Are you willing to risk all for glory?' If your reply is 'Yes', turn to **286**. If it is 'No', turn to **149**.

340

This area proves to be full of rusting, abandoned robots. At the other side of the vault is a huge lift. The control panel has three coloured buttons, but none is marked. The lift contains a huge robot; in the dimness, you cannot make out what type it is, but it has treads and claws. If you enter the lift and push a button at random, turn to **269**. If you take the small corridor beside the lift, turn to **398**.

341

As you speed over the jungle, your instruments warn of an enemy approaching. It is a single Karossean in a captured fighter-craft. He has somehow identified you as a foe; he is already attacking. His robot is a Wasp Fighter, a sleek experimental machine. Only a few exist. It has very little armour, but it has good weapons and handles well.

WASP FIGHTER

ARMOUR 6 SPEED Very Fast SKILL 11

SPECIAL ABILITIES: Whenever the Wasp's Attack Roll exceeds its foe's roll by 4 or more, it has literally flown circles around its foe! It *automatically* wins the *next* combat round – no rolls are necessary.

You cannot *Escape*. If you defeat the Wasp, turn to **137**. If your ARMOUR is reduced to 2, turn to **60**. If your ARMOUR is reduced to 0, you will die in the wreckage of your craft.

342

Down a side-street you hear the sounds of purposeful action. Peering cautiously around the corner, you see that the sounds – banging, clanging noises – are coming from a shop marked 'Robot Repair'. The shop door, naturally, is big enough for a robot to enter, and is invitingly open. If you enter and investigate, turn to **317**. If you go on your way, turn to **110**.

343

They scatter in fear – all but one. He climbs into a large Construction Robot near by and pilots it towards you. If your own robot is faster than Slow, you can *Escape* (turn to **216**). If you would rather fight, turn to **386**.

344

The robot overcomes you and takes the Amulet of Luck away from you. Muttering to itself, it rolls off to be repaired. You lie on the floor, unable to fight further. Lose 2 LUCK points, and reduce your *Initial* LUCK back to its starting score. You struggle back outside to your own robot and climb in. Turn to **396**.

345

Laughing, you scramble into an enemy combat robot! The Myrmidon is the standard Karossean combat robot. It has two forms – humanoid and fighter-plane.

MYRMIDON
Human Form
  ARMOUR 12 SPEED Medium
  COMBAT BONUS +1
Plane Form
  ARMOUR 10 SPEED Very Fast
  COMBAT BONUS +1
  SPECIAL ABILITIES: The Myrmidon can change shape – from humanoid to aircraft, and back.

The Myrmidon takes one combat turn to change forms. During that turn, the robot makes its normal combat roll, but if it wins, it does no damage to the foe – it just defends itself. If you are not in combat, the robot can change shapes freely, with no penalty of any kind – except that if the robot is in humanoid shape and has 2 or less ARMOUR points, it will fall apart if it changes to a plane!

The controls are unfamiliar. If you have read the manual on Karossean robots, turn to 322. If not, turn to 3.

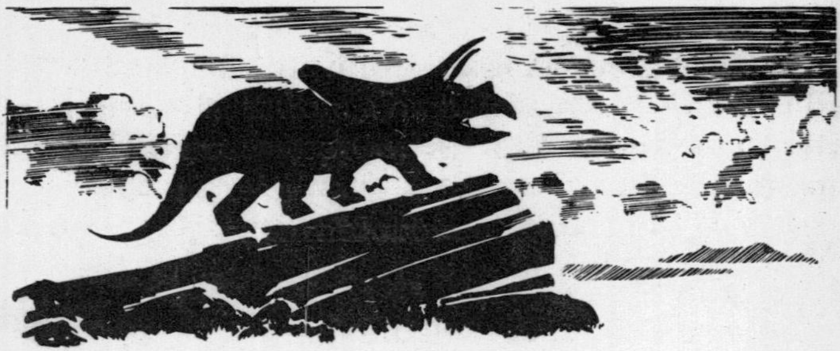

346

With the Cargo Crab, you can carry hundreds of pounds of gold. If you load it up, turn to **287**. If you leave the Treasure House empty-handed (and empty-clawed), turn to **308**.

347

Seconds after you climb back into the robot, it too explodes. Your adventure is over.

348

Your adventure ends here, in the stomach of a dinosaur . . .

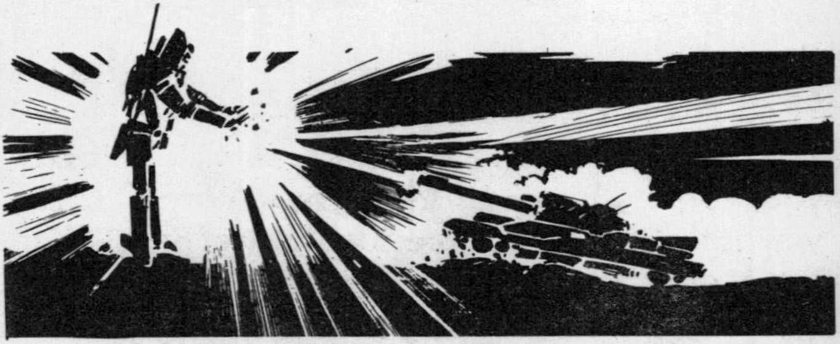

349

You have run into a group of Karosseans patrolling the city! They do not have war machines, but have taken over several of the city's own robots. If your own speed is 'Very Fast', you may escape them *before the battle starts* by leaving the city (turn to **298**). Otherwise, you must fight them one at a time, in order:

STREET CLEANER	ARMOUR 4	SPEED Slow	SKILL 7
TOWING ROBOT	ARMOUR 6	SPEED Medium	SKILL 7
TRAFFIC COPTER	ARMOUR 3	SPEED Fast	SKILL 8

None of these robots has any special abilities. Once the battle starts, you may not *Escape*. If you defeat all three robots, turn to **35**. If your own robot's ARMOUR is reduced to 0, turn to **154**.

350

Test your Luck. If you are Lucky, you make it back to your robot without incident. If you are Unlucky, you trip and fall on the precious flask of Blue Potion. It is broken and lost. You arrive back at your robot just ahead of the pursuing beasts. Turn to **210**.

Gary Mayes.

351

You dive into the water, activating the 'jets' that let your machine swim. You are still in danger – the herd is not just on the land, but thundering through the shallow water as well. But, in the nick of time, you escape them. If you return to the city, turn to **144**. If you try to swim around the herd and investigate the spot where they were originally clustered, turn to **246**.

352

You have defeated your foe. His body vanishes as though it had never existed. Though the temple is silent, you seem to hear victory trumpets. Restore your STAMINA to its *Initial* score, and increase your SKILL and your *Initial* SKILL by 1 (for personal combat only). Return to **166**; you may not visit this temple again.

353

You may fight them one at a time:

	SKILL	STAMINA
First DOCTOR	7	5
Second DOCTOR	6	7
Third DOCTOR	6	5

You cannot *Escape*; you must silence them quickly. If you defeat them, you had better leave the hospital: turn to **308**, collecting your robot on the way, if you have one.

354

You have defeated Minos and his Supertank. Around you is devastation; the few smaller robots you can see are fleeing in panic. The invasion force is routed and broken. You know that in a week or so, your people will recover on their own, and you will be a hero. But right now, all you want is some rest. With none to oppose you, you turn your robot homeward. Your adventure is over . . . and you are victorious!

355

You have slain Minos in fair combat! By ancient custom of the Karosseans, his tribe – the whole Karossean nation – must now submit to your judgement. Needless to say, you order that they awaken your people, and leave your country with all their men and machines. And they do! Before you know it, things are back to normal. Almost . . . One little thing is different. The day on which you defeated Minos is now a national holiday – named after *you*. You are, truly and for ever, a hero.

356

You set off into the jungle, along a path wide enough for a robot – or a dinosaur. Soon the path forks. If you go right, turn to **19**. If you go left, turn to **73**.

357

In the middle of a sentence, your explanations are stilled for ever by the fire from hidden guns. The computer has made a fatal mistake . . . fatal for you as well. Your adventure is over.

358

The Cloak of Invisibility is beginning to flicker. You will not be able to use it again. Before it expires, you make your way out of the Capitol Building and back to your robot. Turn to **308**.

359

If you know the Wasp Fighter's model number, turn to that reference number. If not, turn to **23**.

360

You poke around, looking for something useful. You find nothing, but a huge book falls from a high shelf and hits you on the head. Lose 1 STAMINA point. The other bookshelves are teetering ominously. You leave in disgust and return to the lobby. Turn to **333**.

361

You are in the City of Knowledge. If you have already been here, turn to **40**. Otherwise, keep reading. Here are all of Thalos's greatest universities and museums. This is the home of those who most value learning. Here, you hope, you will find something to help you in your lone struggle. You have a wide choice of possible destinations within the City of Knowledge. Where will you go:

The College of Medicine?	Turn to **54**
The Thalian Museum?	Turn to **14**
The Dinosaur Preserve?	Turn to **66**
The War College?	Turn to **277**
Out of the city?	Turn to **380**

362

You cannot escape in time. A blast nicks your robot's armour. Lose 1 ARMOUR point and wheel to fight your foes. Turn to **169**.

363

As you prepare to leave, it occurs to you that a few bars of this treasure – or, perhaps, more than a few – would be a fair compensation for your troubles so far. If you have taken the Cargo Crab, turn to **346**. If not, turn to **220**.

364

Fortunately, you left the robot building open. You may now return there and get a robot. Turn to **9**.

365

You decide to visit the Temple of Peace. It is a relatively small building in this city of great temples, but easy to find; it is surrounded on all sides by a cool green park. You leave your robot at the edge of the park and walk towards the temple, rather than take a war machine to the Temple of Peace. Somehow, you feel certain that nothing will harm you. The temple is full of sleeping worshippers – but they all wear gentle smiles, and you are sure their dreams are untroubled. You feel moved to pray. What will you pray for:

Complete peace?	Turn to **37**
Strength in battle?	Turn to **390**
Freedom?	Turn to **107**

366

You decide to explore the city. If you explore the northern portion, turn to **16**. If you explore to the south, turn to **225**.

367

Undaunted, you continue towards the City of Industry on foot. *Test your Luck* again. If you are Unlucky, you lose another 3 STAMINA points to exposure. If you are Lucky, you find shelter and water in the wasteland. Eventually, you find a little robot car and finish the trip to the City of Industry. The robot car is a small four-wheeled vehicle, designed for pleasure, but definitely not for combat!

ROBOT CAR

ARMOUR 0 SPEED Fast COMBAT BONUS 0

SPECIAL ABILITIES: This little machine is totally unsuited for fighting! If it is attacked by anything faster, it automatically loses. If attacked by something slower, it can *Escape* if given the chance.

Your car passes through the gates of the City of Industry. Turn to **265**.

368

You realize that you must leave quickly. Looking outside, you see that the Karosseans have entered the building. The fools have left their robots outside and unguarded, parked near yours. You spring out of the window and run for them. If you get back into your own robot, turn to **322**. If you get into a Karossean robot instead, turn to **345**.

369

The lift doors shudder, and the lift drops half a metre and stops. The lights flicker on, and then off. If you push another button, return to **269** and choose again. If you leave the lift and enter the corridor beside it, turn to **398**.

370

You look around the junkyard, and see several things that might be of use. But then you are confronted by a huge creature with the remains of a collar around its neck. It is a Giant Ape, carrying the leg of a robot as though it were a club! At the moment, it seems curious rather than angry. What will you do:

Flee?	Turn to **110**
Speak to the Ape?	Turn to **234**
Attack the Ape?	Turn to **138**

371

If your robot is Very Fast or Fast (ground speed only), turn to **196**. If it is Medium or Slow, turn to **318**.

372

You read through the book one last time . . . and discover an alarming footnote. One of the ingredients you used was Essence of Man-trap Flower. But, according to the footnote, this essence loses its power over time. It may be that the material you used was weak or even totally worthless! The only way to be absolutely certain of success would be either to find some brand-new essence, or to acquire a fresh Man-trap Flower and add it to your flask of Potion. But you have no idea where to look for fresh essence, and the flower itself grows only in the deepest jungle. You pack the fragile bottle of Blue Potion carefully, and set out for your robot. Turn to **302**.

373

You stretch a robot arm to its fullest extension and pluck one of the flowers. The plant shudders. If you possess a Blue Potion, turn to **211**. Otherwise, turn to **248**.

374

You find a stairway and head down. You find that both the Karosseans are dead. One was about your size; you quickly strip off his uniform and put it on yourself. It may come in handy later! You check the signs. The demolished exhibit was labelled 'Tyrannosaurus'. The shouts from outside are coming closer, so you duck out of a convenient door and return to the front desk. Turn to **14**.

375

As you walk down the hallway, you sense eyes boring into your back. Then the doctors run down the hall away from you, shouting! Evidently your accent gave you away. You cannot catch them; you hurriedly flee from the hospital and back to the place where you left your robot (if you have a robot). Lose 1 STAMINA point. Turn to **308**.

376

You are leaving the City of the Guardians. If you decide to go to the City of Storms, turn to **144**. If you decide to go to the City of Industry, turn to **265**.

377

Your opponent falls, mortally wounded. A gasp goes up from the circle of officers watching the battle. As you reel back, one of them catches you. You see Minos dusting off his hands and drawing his sword. 'Here! Drink this!' says the Karossean officer who kept you from falling. If you drink the flask he offers, turn to **388**. If you decline, turn to **330**.

378

You are leaving the City of Pleasure. If you would like to go to the City of Industry, turn to **265**. If you would like to go to the City of the Jungle, turn to **274**.

379

To your horror, you are caught in a downdraught! Your robot falls, spinning. You are thrown against the side of the cockpit. Around you, metal shrieks. Lose 2 STAMINA points; your robot loses 2 ARMOUR points. If either STAMINA or ARMOUR is reduced to 0, you are dead. If not, you have a chance to regain control. Turn to **12**.

380

You are leaving the City of Knowledge . . . hopefully, wiser than when you came. Where will you travel now:

The City of Industry?	Turn to **265**
The City of the Jungle?	Turn to **137**
The City of Storms?	Turn to **179**
The City of Worship?	Turn to **166**

381

Without their pilots, the other robots are defenceless. Your own machine quickly hammers them into junk. But as you attack the last one, it fights back! Evidently it was left on autopilot. Your own robot loses 3 ARMOUR points before you can destroy that last foe. You leave the War College at top speed, with the Karossean pilots shouting angrily behind you from the windows. But you have lost part of the advantage of surprise; the Karosseans now know that at least one person remains awake to oppose their scheme! Turn to **147**.

382

Lose 2 LUCK points for abandoning the sleepers to the tender mercies of the hungry dinosaur. If you have not already explored the south of the city, you may do so (turn to **225**). Otherwise, turn to **137**.

383

You wander around for hours, but the Administration Building is useless, and the other building is tightly locked and you cannot enter it. You must leave the Dinosaur Preserve and see what you can find. Unfortunately, the Dinosaur Preserve is far away from the rest of the City of Knowledge. After an hour of walking, the best you have been able to find is a battered old Farm Robot.

FARM ROBOT

ARMOUR 7 SPEED Medium COMBAT BONUS 0
SPECIAL ABILITIES: None

But it is better than nothing, so you take it. Turn to **150**.

384

You are caught in the remains of your robot as the Crusher's enormous foot comes down one last time. Your end is mercifully quick.

385

You have arrived at the National Treasure House. A great, grey building, it is the repository of all Thalos's gold. To your surprise, it is guarded only by a single Karossean sentry, standing in front of the building. If you have a robot, turn to **319**. If you are on foot, turn to **271**.

Gary Mayes.

386

The enemy Construction Robot raises huge claws and moves towards you. It rolls on eight vast wheels. It has only a few guns, to protect against attacking dinosaurs, but it has four huge arms mounted all around.

CONSTRUCTION ROBOT
ARMOUR 9 SPEED Slow SKILL 6
SPECIAL ABILITIES: None

Fortunately for you, the Karossean soldier inside does not really know how to use this robot. If the two dice you roll for the Construction Robot ever total 6 or less, turn to **194**. If you *Escape*, turn to **216**. If you defeat the Construction Robot, turn to **92**. If your own robot's ARMOUR is reduced to 0, turn to **61**.

387

The placid beasts are quite familiar with robots; they honk and hiss, but move over to let you through. Turn to **62**.

388

You drink. A tingling goes through your body. 'You put up a good show!' says the officer in a whisper. 'By law, you shouldn't have to duel Minos until you can rest, but he's coming for you right now. This will even the odds.' You thank him for his sportsmanship. Obviously not all Karosseans are totally bad! The officer's healing drink gives you 4 STAMINA points, or restores you to your *Initial* STAMINA, whichever is less. Turn to **330**.

389

The Karosseans fire on you. Lose 1 ARMOUR point and fight. Turn to **169**.

390

The room somehow seems colder. The feeling of peace evaporates (lose 1 LUCK point). Quickly you rise and walk back to your robot. You realize that your request was inappropriate. Return to **166**; you may not visit this temple again.

391

Your luck has run out! The Tyrannosaurus spots you and gobbles you up in a second. Your adventure is over – and a short one it was, too.

392

Exploring the second floor, you find several prototype models of an odd-looking helmet. According to the files you read there, it is an Interface Transponder. While you wear one of these helmets, increase your SKILL by 1 when using a robot, up to a maximum SKILL of 11. That is, if your SKILL is already 11 or 12, it does not help you. It does not affect other combats. If you leave the Centre and return to your robot outside, turn to **206**. If you want to explore further, return to **333** and make another selection.

393

You step into the game and pick up the toy ray-gun that comes with it. A light comes on and you see yourself in a mirror – but a holographic trick has clothed your reflection in a beard and a Karossean uniform. You laugh and fire at it. Unfortunately, with all the repairmen sleeping, this machine is out of order. When you fire, you receive a severe electrical shock. Roll one die. On 1, 2 or 3, you lose 1 point of SKILL. On 4, 5 or 6, you lose 1 point of STAMINA. If you want to play another game, turn to **288**. If you want to leave the Arcade, turn to **165**.

394

You pack the fragile bottle of Blue Potion carefully, and set out for your robot. Turn to **302**.

395

You dash down the hallway, following the signs marked 'Library'. You turn a corner and run headlong into a Karossean guard! You finish him off before he can summon aid, but he wounds you slightly: lose 1 STAMINA point. Once at the library, you ransack it for information on sleeping sickness. But you find nothing; the relevant volumes are all missing. You realize this has been a wild-goose chase. Carefully, you slip out of the hospital and away. Return to **308**.

396

You are leaving the Thalian Museum. Where would you like to go now:

The College of War?	Turn to **277**
The Dinosaur Preserve?	Turn to **66**
The College of Medicine?	Turn to **54**
Out of the city?	Turn to **380**

397

After a few hours, the door opens and a soldier tosses in a package of rations. Desperately, you grab his arm before the door closes! The Karossean tumbles to the floor. He has no chance against your berserk rage. You leave him unconscious, at a cost of 2 STAMINA points to yourself. In an adjoining room, you find your sword lying underneath a table, but there is no sign of your other Possessions. If you search for them, turn to **174**. If you leave immediately, turn to **69**.

398

The corridor levels off and passes a small alcove. Within the alcove is a small lift, just big enough for one person. If you want to get in the lift and press the button, turn to **307**. If you continue along the corridor, turn to **178**.

399

You speed away. Behind you, the Karossean pilots come charging out of the building, heading for their robots. But you know the city better than they do; though they hunt for you, your head start is enough to see you safely away. But you have lost part of the advantage of surprise; the Karosseans now know that at least one person remains awake to oppose their scheme! Turn to **147**.

400

You fight the Ankylosaurus. This small but powerful dinosaur is studded with armour-plate. Its tail is tipped with a huge ball of bone which it swings like a mace.

ANKYLOSAURUS

ARMOUR 12 SPEED Slow SKILL 9

SPECIAL ABILITIES: If your robot has two or four legs and the Ankylosaurus hits you, it will knock you off your feet. This does no extra damage. However, on the next turn, if you hit the Ankylosaurus you will do it no damage. You have only defended yourself against it.

If you *Escape*, turn to **115**. If you defeat the Ankylosaurus, turn to **56**. If your robot is destroyed, you are lost in the jungle and your adventure is over.

Also in Puffins

Steve Jackson's

SORCERY!

1: THE SHAMUTANTI HILLS

Your search for the legendary Crown of Kings takes you to the Shamutanti Hills. Alive with evil creatures, lawless wanderers and bloodthirsty monsters, the land is riddled with tricks and traps waiting for the unwary traveller. Will you be able to cross the hills safely and proceed to the second part of the adventure – or will you perish in the attempt?

2: KHARÉ – CITYPORT OF TRAPS

As a warrior relying on force of arms, or a wizard trained in magic, you must brave the terror of a city built to trap the unwary. You will need all your wits about you to survive the unimaginable horrors ahead and to make sense of the clues which may lead to your success – or to your doom!

3: THE SEVEN SERPENTS

Seven deadly and magical serpents speed ahead of you to warn the evil Archmage of your coming. Will you be able to catch them before they get there?

4: THE CROWN OF KINGS

At the end of your long trek, you face the unknown terrors of the Mampang Fortress. Hidden inside the keep is the Crown of Kings – the ultimate goal of the *Sorcery!* epic. But beware! For if you have not defeated the Seven Serpents, your arrival has been anticipated . . .

Complete with all the magical spells you will need, each book can be played either on its own or as part of the whole epic.

THE CRETAN CHRONICLES

BLOODFEUD OF ALTHEUS
AT THE COURT OF KING MINOS
RETURN OF THE WANDERER

John Butterfield, David Honigmann, Philip Parker

Set in the mythological world of Ancient Greece, this 3-book epic brings an exciting historical dimension to Adventure Gamebooks. YOU are Altheus, sent to avenge the death of Theseus, your elder brother, whose body lies trapped in the labyrinth of King Minos. The combat system has been extended to incorporate the concepts of honour and shame.

MAELSTROM

Alexander Scott

Complete with beginners' and advanced rules, referee's notes, maps and charts. *Maelstrom* is a full role-playing game for several players. YOU choose the characters, YOU decide the missions and YOU have the adventures in the turbulent world of Europe in the sixteenth century.

Fantasy Questbooks – 32 pages, full colour

THE PATH OF PERIL

David Fickling and Perry Hinton

Illustrated by Rachel Birkett

The famous explorer, Edmund Mallory, has been foully murdered, and the legendary Bloodstone, which he acquired under mysterious circumstances on his last travels, is missing. All that remains are the scattered fragments of the explorer's diary, his personal notebook and most of the contents of his ransacked study. An almost unsolvable mystery. Yet it seems that the explorer himself expected to meet a violent end and prepared the way for YOU to track down his murderer and recover the Bloodstone. Unfortunately the clues he laid have been scattered in the turmoil of his terrible death. All the information you need is here, ingeniously hidden in both text and pictures, and each strand of the mystery unravels to reveal the next. Are YOU sharp enough to crack it?

STARFLIGHT ZERO

David Fickling and Perry Hinton

Illustrated by Peter Andrew Jones

One by one the Free Planets have fallen to the relentless advance of the Dark Ships until only Caldoran and Palonar remain. Then a last, despairing message comes from Palonar and Caldoran is on its own. It seems that the invaders, armed with the power of the invincible Black Light, will soon conquer the last outpost of resistance. The only hope for the survival of Caldoran is one last desperate mission by a small group of star fighters to strike at the source of the Black Light. And YOU are part of the mission.